STEPHANIE HARVEY • ANNIE W
MAGGIE HODDINOTT • SUZANNE CARROLL

Intervention Reinvention

A Volume-Based Approach to Reading Success

SCHOLASTIC

*To Dr. Mary Howard, who teaches us that
interventions must be planned with care
and implemented with love.*

*To Dr. Teri Lesesne, who shows us
the power of relentless book-matching.*

*In your honor, we keep children and books
close at heart always.*

Publisher/Content editor: Lois Bridges
Editorial director: Sarah Longhi
Editor-in-chief/Development editor: Raymond Coutu
Senior editor: Shelley Griffin
Production editor: Danny Miller
Designer: Maria Lilja

Photos ©: cover boy: alejandrophotography/Getty Images; cover tree: Dudarev Mikhail/Shutterstock; cover sky: Iakov Kalinin/Shutterstock; 63 top left and right: courtesy of Areceli Cerda; 63 bottom left: courtesy of Elodia Miranda; 63 bottom right: courtesy of Jennifer Gonzalez. All other photos courtesy of the authors.

Pages from *Diary of a Pug: Pug Blasts Off* text copyright © 2019 by Scholastic Inc., illustrations copyright © 2019 by Kyla May. Used by permission of Scholastic Inc.; *Dragon Masters: Future of the Time Dragon* text copyright © 2020 by Tracey West, illustrations by Daniel Griffo copyright © 2020 by Scholastic Inc. Used by permission of Scholastic Inc.; *Scholastic Discover More: Weather* by Penelope Arlon and Tory Gordon-Harris copyright © 2013 by Scholastic Inc.; *The Notebook of Doom: Rise of the Balloon Goons* text and illustrations copyright © 2013 by Troy Cummings. Used by permission of Scholastic Inc.; *The Baby-Sitters Club: Kristy's Big Day* text copyright © 2018 by Ann M. Martin, illustrations copyright © 2018 by Gale Galligan. Used by permission of Scholastic Inc.; *Twins* text copyright © 2020 by Varian Johnson, illustrations copyright © 2020 by Shannon Wright. Used by permission of Scholastic Inc.; *Amulet: Prince of the Elves* text and illustrations copyright © 2012 by Kazu Kibuishi. Used by permission of Scholastic Inc. and Hansen Literary Management, LLC. Panel from *Missile Mouse: The Star Crusher* text and illustrations copyright © 2010 by Jake Parker. Used by permission of Scholastic Inc. and Hansen Literary Management, LLC.
All rights reserved.

1 2 3 4 5 6 7 8 9 10   40   30 29 28 27 26 25 24 23 22 21

Scholastic Inc., 557 Broadway, New York, NY 10012

CONTENTS

ACKNOWLEDGMENTS

We write these words one year into the devastating global pandemic. Above all, we wish to honor educators everywhere who mobilized in an instant to reassure, guide, and teach children through the crisis. We salute you with boundless respect.

We thank our editor extraordinaire, Lois Bridges, for over-the-top enthusiasm and wise guidance. Throughout this project, our phones would ping and light up with Lois's 3:00 a.m. emails brimming with affirmation, research nuggets, and practical suggestions. Lois cares deeply about literacy and recognizes that reading is a path to a life of bright ideas and spirited actions.

We are deeply indebted to the creative, patient, and flexible Scholastic team that kept us on track and on time, knitting together and refining our ideas at each stage of the process: Ray Coutu, Sarah Longhi, Shelley Griffin, Danny Miller, and Maria Lilja.

We are proud to capture the work of educators in Mamaroneck, New York, who are committed to increasing reading volume and guiding children on the upward spiral to reading success: Board of Education trustees, Superintendent Dr. Robert Shaps, teachers, administrators, and student-support personnel. We are particularly grateful to coaches Laurie Pastore, Mariana Ivanov, and Jesse Dancy, and to Giovanna Mascoli, for their relentless commitment to kids. And a special shout-out goes to district purchasing agent, Lauren Leone, for establishing nimble procedures that let teachers put the right books in kids' hands right away.

Steph thanks her husband, kids, and grandkids who give her aspirational hope about this work going forward, as well as for the future of the planet.

Annie thanks her entire blended family for their interest and support, especially Bill, Mimi, Nick, and Sanka.

Maggie thanks her children—Jake, Cooper, and Matthew—for the laughs, hugs, and inspiration. She also thanks pod-mates Jory, Matt, and Eliana for inviting the boys on many pandemic playdates so she could write in peace. Above all, she thanks her husband, Mike, for his endless support and encouragement.

Suzanne thanks her entire family for their love and support, especially her mother, Dr. Mary Byrne, for showing her what a strong woman is capable of, her children, Charlotte and Shane, for making each day an adventure, and her husband, Ed, for being a true partner in this life.

Finally, we'd like to thank authors and illustrators, editors and publishers, and kids and families who read and write for a better world. Author/illustrator Jess Keating said it best in a recent Tweet: "I know we talk a lot about books being windows and doors, but this pandemic has shown us that books can also be shelters. Sometimes you just need to live between the covers for a while, and I'm really glad to be in a business that creates the necessary space for people."

Greetings Readers

In *Intervention Reinvention*, we dive into the power of reading volume to help you grow confident, capable readers. Because everyone deserves a rich reading life, we reconsider traditional intervention models, keeping the following in mind:

- **The Power of Volume.** In 2017, Annie and Steph authored *From Striving to Thriving: How to Grow Confident, Capable Readers*, which emphasizes that the more kids read, the better they read. *Intervention Reinvention* shares volume-building strategies and book-matching techniques that build on that foundation in the intervention landscape.

- **Teacher as Decision Maker.** We wade into the fascinating, uncharted waters of the decisions teachers make in their daily interactions with children. We explore how the choices teachers make, informed by kidwatching and conferring, can ensure that striving readers experience high-success reading.

- **Equity and Social Justice.** It is well known that children of color and children in poverty are overrepresented in intervention settings. It is also clear that too few texts reflect their daily life experience. We have a moral imperative to provide them with high-quality in-class instruction and enthralling, relevant reading materials. It is an issue of social justice.

- **Inclusive Pronoun Use.** You will notice the inclusion of *they* as a singular, gender-neutral pronoun. While this may look and sound incorrect, the dichotomous use of *he* and *she* excludes those who do not identify with gender-specific pronouns. We choose to alternate between all three.

This book is for anyone who supports children's literacy development in grades 2–8. The strategies we suggest are particularly effective with students who have moved beyond the early stages of reading development. We recognize that you likely have a curriculum in place for word study, assessment, and skill-focused intervention. Volume, however, is often the missing element in that curriculum. So please, let them read!

Our approach is not prescriptive. There are many pathways to successful reading; we reject one-size-fits-all instruction. We aim to mediate the conditions that enable kids to learn, thrive, and ultimately love to read. Thank you for jumping in with us!

—Steph, Annie, Maggie, and Suzanne

How This Book Is Organized

Intervention Reinvention invites you to extend and amplify your instruction with volume-based interventions. It shows you how to pump up the amount of reading your students do because, as we know, one of the best ways to become a better reader is by reading.

PART I offers the foundational information you need to launch your students on an upward spiral to reading success. For children who are not yet thriving as readers, we advocate for and describe actions for designing, implementing, and tracking volume-building interventions to improve their reading skills.

The Virtuous Cycle
(page 15)

Transforming Response to Intervention *(page 49)*

Nine Actions That Promote Voluminous Reading

By thoughtfully curating her classroom library, Lorraine created conditions for striving reader Brianna to thrive. She also set up the rest of her class to read successfully and independently. In Part II, which provides the tools to support individual readers intensively, you'll notice that we periodically redirect you back to this chapter to make sure you're embracing critical, foundational actions. When you do, you equip most kids to read voluminously, which enables you to focus your volume-building attention on those kids who need it most.

Know Kids in the Round

Because children thrive when they feel known and valued, building genuine and trusting relationships is the core of our work. In a profound essay in *The Teacher You Want to Be*, Katherine Bomer urges that we view students "with an air of expectancy," taking an open, inquisitive, and appreciative stance as we get to know them over time: "Notice that the actions of looking, listening, and accepting require us to change our stance in the classroom from being the constant deliverer of information, source of all answers, and evaluator and judge...to becoming curious, empathetic, and accepting of what *is* in our students" (2015).

The following prompts help you get to know each of your students and focus your teaching accordingly. For example, from informal conversations, Lorraine knew that Brianna had two older brothers at home, who were thriving readers of chapter books. From queries from Brianna's mother, she knew to use in two ways: 1. She assured Brianna's parents that the Little People, BIG DREAMS biographies Brianna was reading were appropriately meaty. 2. She suspected that Brianna would seek hefty books to keep up with her brothers and classmates, and would need to find thick yet accessible anthologies to fit the bill.

Know a Child as a Person
- Who are the important people in his life? What are their occupations, schedules, and preferred modes of communication?
- Are other language(s) spoken at home?
- What are the child's interests? What does he know and care a lot about? Does he play a sport, belong to a club, or pursue a hobby?
- What responsibilities (chores, sibling care, job) does he have beyond schoolwork?
- Who are his friends?

Know a Child as a Learner
- What have his prior school experiences been like?
- What curricular topics interest him most? Least?
- Does he prefer to collaborate or work independently?
- Does he have reliable access to tech tools and the Internet outside of school?
- What is his level of academic self-confidence?

Nine Actions That Promote Voluminous Reading *(pages 25–45)*

PART II provides tools with which to study your students and identify those who would benefit from your immediate attention. Then, with specific students in mind, it explains how to use the Volume Decision Tree to ask and answer diagnostic questions and pinpoint instructional options to increase their reading volume.

Volume Decision Tree
(pages 72–73)

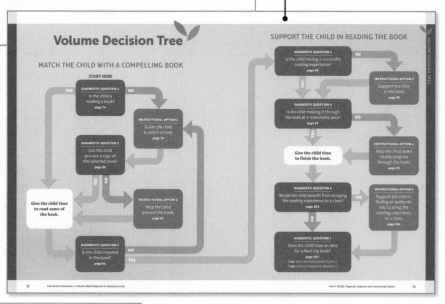

The Volume Decision Tree contains seven Diagnostic Questions to help you assess specific areas of need to put the child on the path to high-success, voluminous reading.

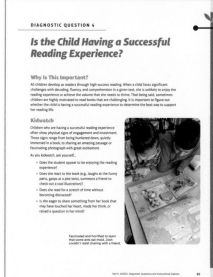

Each Diagnostic Question has a related set of Instructional Options. Using data you collect through kidwatching and conferring, you choose from the Instructional Options to meet the child's needs. Then you return to the Volume Decision Tree and proceed to the next Diagnostic Question.

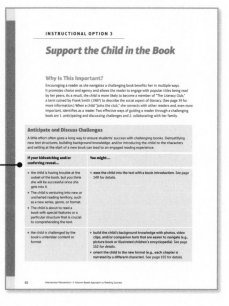

Part III contains responsive practices—practical ways to increase the amount of reading your students do daily. You'll find ideas for matching children with compelling books, supporting them as they read those books, and putting them on the upward spiral described in Part I.

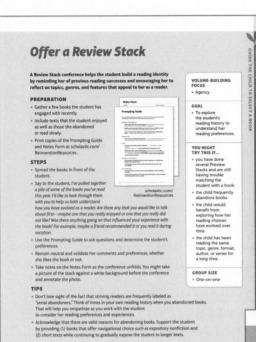

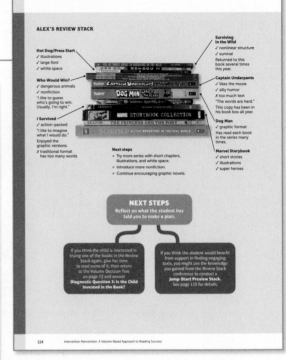

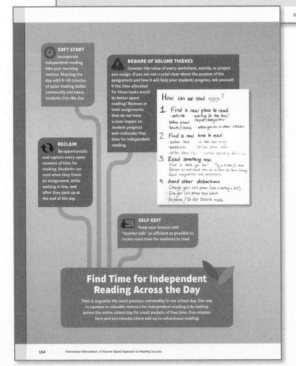

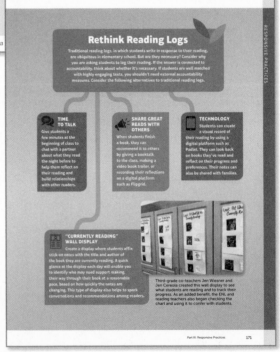

Part I

A Volume-Based Approach to Reading Success

In Part I, we invite you to learn about the virtuous cycle in which children flourish by turning page after page in books that they love. To guide you in launching your students on that upward spiral to reading success, we describe a series of practical actions for you to take in your classroom. In addition, for those children who are not yet thriving as readers, we advocate for and describe how to design, implement, and track volume-building interventions.

 Visit **scholastic.com/ReinventionResources** for downloadable forms, videos with the authors, and more!

CHAPTER 1

Volume and Capability: The Virtuous Cycle

Third-grade teacher Andrew Figueroa watched Tara during reading workshop as she read *Sable*, a chapter book by Karen Hesse. Andrew knew the book hadn't come from his classroom library, so he assumed Tara had brought it from home. Although she had turned to the book on three consecutive days, Tara wasn't progressing through it, popping her head up frequently to scan the room. Andrew conferred with her and invited her to read a little with him. Tara read a passage haltingly, looking to Andrew several times for guidance with unfamiliar words and dialect.

Although Andrew had read many of Hesse's books, he had not read *Sable*. He noted its 1994 publication date, rural mountain setting, and lyrical language—factors that likely posed challenges for Tara in spite of an enticing new-edition cover and storyline of a young girl seeking to adopt a stray dog. Although Tara expressed interest in continuing with *Sable* during their conference, Andrew was concerned that it would not be a high-success reading experience.

Andrew emailed Tara's mother to share his observations and seek input. Perhaps she would know the reason Tara chose *Sable* that he should keep in mind. Tara's mother responded right away, grateful for the outreach. "At home it is very difficult to get [Tara] to commit to a book and read for a sustained period of time," she wrote, adding, "I'm becoming increasingly concerned that this might be some sort of processing challenge." Andrew and Tara's mom agreed on a plan that would honor her interest in *Sable*: at home, mom would read and discuss the book with Tara; at school, Andrew would help Tara chunk it and take stock after reading each chunk. Andrew also said he would introduce Tara to a few more accessible options for her Next-Up book.

A few days later, Andrew assembled a Preview Stack of books, using the technique he had learned from Maggie and Suzanne in an in-service course. He included titles from several popular series, along with some nonfiction on high-interest topics. As he presented each option, Andrew gauged Tara's interest. She left the Preview Stack conference with several "yes" books in her basket, one of which she began to read right away. As Andrew monitored Tara's engagement with the books she had selected, he continued to provide her with small-group instruction on self-monitoring and decoding multisyllabic words, skills he had assessed as particular areas of challenge.

Andrew wrote to update Tara's mother:

"I had the opportunity to meet with Tara to help her find books more suited to her and to create a reading plan. We went through a few books, and she selected some that she wanted to read. She put three in her book basket and added two more to the list in her notebook. Besides *Heidi Heckelbeck,* which you probably have seen, she chose *Dory Fantasmagory* and *Bea Garcia: My Life in Pictures*. She is reading the first Heidi Heckelbeck book this week and is on pace to finish soon. She also took out the second book in the series. (There are about 20 of them.) She seems to be liking them, and we will continue to meet to talk about them. These books should also work well for Tara to apply the skills we have been working on in class during the last few weeks. She also decided to put *Sable* on hold for a bit."

For the next few weeks, Tara blazed through the Heidi Heckelbeck series, reading the books in rapid succession. Her mother reported that Tara was reading at home voluntarily and withdrew an earlier request she had made for an intervention conference with Andrew and the school's reading specialist. When Andrew assessed Tara formally, he confirmed that she had made substantial gains, reaching the district's mid-year independent reading level benchmark for third grade.

Informally, Andrew noted that Tara began dropping in around lunchtime to talk to him about the Heidi Heckelbeck books, speaking of the characters as if they were real people in her life. She also began connecting with classmates who were into the series and recommending it to others.

The Upward Spiral to Success

Tara's remarkable reading growth was no accident. It was the result of Andrew's careful monitoring of her independent reading life, beginning with observing that she was not progressing through the book she had chosen. In addition to the reading comprehension strategies that he was teaching in whole-class and small-group lessons, and the syllabication work he was doing with Tara, Andrew explored Tara's level of investment in the book, while exposing her to other possibilities. He book-matched with great success, drawing on his classroom library collection that he had curated over time with Maggie's support.

Andrew's book-matching efforts constituted a volume-based intervention, one that propelled Tara from a reading stall to a spiral of high-success reading. She not only moved to a higher independent reading level, but also developed a reading identity and gained overall confidence.

In this chapter, we show you how to enter students into a virtuous cycle where they flourish as readers and put our instruction to effective and authentic use. This is urgent, necessary work; without it, readers may follow a reverse path on which they fall behind and lose their identities as readers. Once we explain the way the spiral works, we explore volume itself: the impact of "home-run" and "watershed" books, how much reading we want kids to do, what kind of pace we generally expect from them at various grades, and how the type of reading they're doing and other factors contribute to their reading volume.

Setting the Spiral in Motion

In the following sections, we discuss how to launch the cycle, get students reading, set expectations and measure volume, and track growth.

Launch the Virtuous Cycle

Tara's progress can be attributed to the virtuous cycle, a well-known concept to reading researchers. Cunningham and Stanovich (1998) assert that "Reading has cognitive consequences that extend beyond its immediate task of lifting meaning from a particular passage. Furthermore, those consequences are reciprocal and exponential in nature. Accumulated over time—spiraling either upward or downward—they carry profound implications for the development of a wide range of cognitive capabilities." Similarly, Stanovich (1986) cites the "Matthew effects" in reading, inspired by the biblical passage in which the "rich get richer" and the "poor get poorer," by reading a lot or little, respectively.

Children who read capably feel good about reading and about themselves as readers. Their success motivates them to read more. As they read, they draw pleasure from the text and gain navigational experience; they acquire vocabulary and develop background knowledge; and they continue to grow as readers. In describing the upward spiral, Guthrie and Barber (2013) state, "In and out of school, people like things they do well."

This graphic depicts the virtuous cycle in which reading volume, success, confidence, and capability grow together in an upward spiral. Powerful benefits of this cycle—such as curiosity, knowledge, empathy, adventurousness, and agency—spring forth and extend beyond the act of reading to enrich and expand the reader. Although this may sound too good to be true, we have seen daily, incremental growth in our students when we've entered them into the cycle, even our most striving students. Tara is a good example. Not only did she become a more capable reader but also, in the words of Peter Johnston (2013) she became "the kind of person who" relishes talking about books with peers and adults.

Of course, the opposite is true, with devastating results. Children who have a hard time learning to read avoid reading because it makes them feel unsuccessful and inadequate. That avoidance diminishes their reading volume, which, in turn, diminishes their reading growth. Once that downward spiral is set in motion, striving readers fall behind and often find themselves in texts that are too challenging (as *Sable* was for Tara), which only exacerbates their feelings of inadequacy and avoidance behaviors. Author Jon Scieszka refers to that as the reading "death spiral." In a *Washington Post* interview (Strauss, 2008), he explains, "It's where kids aren't reading and then are worse at reading because they aren't reading, and then they read less because it is hard and they get worse, and then they see themselves as non-readers, and it's such a shame" (2009). And, as our editor. Lois Bridges, puts it, "It's not just a shame; it's a disaster. Readers often get caught in a downward spiral from which they never recover" (2010). According to Cunningham and Stanovich, "We should provide all children, regardless of their achievement levels, with as many reading experiences as possible. Indeed, this becomes doubly imperative for precisely those children whose verbal abilities are most in need of bolstering, for it is the very act of reading that can build those capacities" (1998). For that reason, jump-starting our students' reading lives—particularly our striving students' reading lives—and then seeing to it that they engage in daily, voluminous, high-success reading is job #1!

The Virtuous Cycle

CONFIDENCE

Participates in reading community; reads deeply and widely in realms of interest

EMPATHY

IDENTITY

Uses literacy actions to solve problems

Reads a lot! Progresses from books with high-frequency and/or decodable words and predictable structures to books with more sophisticated elements and features

SELF-ADVOCACY

Acquires useful knowledge to enrich life. Infers meaning; ponders the text between reading installments; seeks out others for text-based discussions

ADVENTURE

RISK-TAKING

Savors the feeling of evolving competence; seeks opportunities to read independently and to others

Applies emerging sound-symbol correspondences to decode words

CURIOSITY

Turns pages on cue; recites familiar lines

KNOWLEDGE

Recognizes words on sight

Develops concepts of print

AGENCY

Relishes longer and more complex texts

Points at illustrations

CAPABILITY

Grasps connections between spoken and written language

Requests to be read to

PLEASURE

Chooses favorite books and learns how to handle them

MOTIVATION

Internalizes literary language and story structure

The Power of Confidence

Steph's granddaughter Riley, age six as of this writing, has loved reading since she was born. When her parents, grandparents, and teachers read to her as a toddler, she always begged for more. She went to preschool over the moon about learning to read and making new friends, which she did happily. Enter Stella, Riley's BFF, a darling child who happened to read proficiently by age four. Proficient reading happens at that young age—not often, but now and then.

As a reading specialist, Steph is well aware that it's almost impossible to distinguish later in life a student who learned to read by preschool and one who learned in second grade, but Riley made the distinction. When Steph took the two girls to the Museum of Nature and Science, Stella, casually and seemingly unconsciously, read practically all of the signage about the T.Rex. Riley grew quieter than usual that morning. When Steph brought her home, for the first time ever, she didn't beg for an Elephant and Piggie book.

Reading is first and foremost about confidence. The subtitle for Steph and Annie's *From Striving to Thriving* is *How to Grow Confident, Capable Readers. Confident* comes before

capable because, simply put, there is no capability without confidence. In fact, confidence builds capability. The more confident a reader, the more capable he or she becomes; the more capable he or she is, the more confidence grows, leading to a virtuous cycle rather than a vicious cycle (Pearson, 2014).

Guthrie (2013) recognizes three powerful motivators that drive student reading—interest, confidence, and dedication. Of confidence, he explains, "Believing in yourself is more closely linked to achievement than any other motivation throughout school. Confidence, which is belief in your capacity, is tied intimately to success." Striving readers usually don't believe in themselves as learners and, instead, believe they are less competent than they really are.

Fortunately, Riley overcame her lack of confidence. Reading was simply too compelling for her to give up on it. But Steph had to pay attention to Riley's experience and respond sensitively. It serves as a lesson for us about how easily confidence can erode. Some tips for building confidence follow.

- Table the labels in your school and classroom. Nothing saps confidence more quickly than being labeled a *slow, poor, low,* and/or *challenged learner*. Lose the labels yesterday. See *From Striving to Thriving*, Chapter 1, for much more on this topic.

- Share something you are good at and feel confident about. Explain how doing the activity makes you feel and why it makes you feel that way. Then explore with kids something they love to do and that makes them feel confident. We need for them to understand what confidence is, how it makes us feel, and how it can make us more capable learners.

- Share your challenges with reading as well as your successes. Show yourself confused by a word or idea in a text, and then model how you overcome the hurdle. Children often think adults have all the answers. Let them know that reading can be tough for you, too, but that you always attempt to work your way through, even though it may be frustrating at first.

- Refer to mistakes as attempts. We want strivers to embrace their mistakes, but the word *mistake* is loaded, and strivers are all too familiar with mistake making because, over time, they are likely to have made more than their fair share. So how about replacing the word *mistake* with the word *attempt? Attempt* has a less pejorative connotation. The word does not carry the baggage that comes with *mistake*.

Connect Children With Home-Run Books and Create Watershed Reading Experiences

In our experience with children like Tara, a single successful reading experience has the power to launch the upward spiral, and research bears that out as well. While writing *From Striving to Thriving: How to Grow Confident, Capable Readers* (2017), Annie and Steph took a deep dive into that research.

HOME-RUN BOOKS

Jim Trelease, prior to the 2001 publication of his landmark *Read-Aloud Handbook*, hypothesized in personal correspondence with Dr. Stephen Krashen that a single powerful reading experience— the reading of a "home-run" book—was powerful enough to spark a permanent interest in reading. In 2000, Krashen and colleagues conducted several studies to test Trelease's hypothesis by asking students whether they enjoyed reading—and, if they did, the researchers went on to ask them if they could identify a particular book that had first grabbed them, a "home-run" book. Von Sprecken, Kim, and Krashen found that 53 percent of fourth graders queried had had a home-run reading experience, and Kim and Krashen found that 75 percent of sixth graders had, too. The phenomenon is real!

However, further research indicates that while a home-run experience might lead to a permanent interest in reading, it does not guarantee it. In 2002, Ujiie and Krashen studied 266 fourth and fifth graders to determine whether students who reported having a home-run experience continued to enjoy reading. They also studied whether the experience was the result of reading "quality literature."

- Ujiie and Krashen found that 82 percent of students could identify a home-run book and that most of them reported that they continued to enjoy reading. However, they found that a substantial number of students felt indifferent about reading, in spite of having had a home-run experience. "Having a home-run experience typically leads to greater reading interest, but does not guarantee it," Ujiie and Krashen concluded.

- Additionally, they found that "it was difficult to characterize home-run books, because, as in other studies, children named a wide variety of home-run books. Very few titles were selected by more than a handful of students. None of the books ever won a Newbery, Caldecott, or Bluebonnet award. Three were on the list of the 100 most challenged books of 1990–1999."

Research on home-run books has many important implications for our work.

- Readers' tastes are quirky and idiosyncratic, and they warrant our respect. When a child leans into or away from a book, we should notice it without judgment. "Expose, don't impose," as Mamaroneck literacy specialist Ginny Lockwood advises.

- "Lowbrow" books play a huge role in many readers' development. While award-winning titles may attract our attention, we need to acknowledge that they may not necessarily have the kid appeal to launch and sustain the virtuous cycle. "When I read Garfield books in first grade, I thought I found something better than TV." So opens the 2000 study cited above.

- Home-run books are often reread repeatedly. Here in Mamaroneck, many readers who have made accelerated growth have also checked out the same books over and over from school libraries, often to the chagrin of teachers and parents. We need to recognize that rereading is an indicator of high engagement that is likely propelling the reader upward on the spiral. (See Explore the Benefits of Lingering in Comfortable or Familiar Books, page 123.)

- We mustn't become complacent when a child has a home-run reading experience. We must continue book-matching relentlessly to ensure progress. Otherwise, readers may have "strike-out experiences" with books that could dampen or even derail their upward momentum. For example, Maggie's brother Andrew fondly remembers reading the entire Harry Potter series back-to-back but has since lamented, "Those were the only books I ever enjoyed reading."

WATERSHED READING EXPERIENCES

Because home-run book experiences can be unpredictable in terms of outcomes, we have coined the term "watershed" reading experience as the gold standard. A watershed reading experience unleashes a continuous and sustained flow of engaged reading, rather than discrete episodes. As was true in Tara's case, series books are often the source of watershed reading experiences. Their familiar characters and settings set readers up for surefire success from page one.

When we ask workshop participants, "What vivid and voluminous experiences do you remember from childhood?," series books are mentioned most often and reverently. We laugh as participants date themselves by revealing whether it was Cherry Ames, Nancy Drew, The Baby-Sitters Club, or Goosebumps that launched their passion for reading.

Among the many brilliant essays in *Making the Match* (2003) is one by poet Paul Janeczko called "The Hardy Boys Made Me Do It," in which he describes the life-altering discovery of his first Hardy Boys mystery at a flea market:

> "When I read the opening pages of that novel, I knew I was onto something. It was as if my teachers had been teaching me to read by looking through the wrong end of the telescope. But when I read my first Hardy Boys book, it was as if Frank and Joe had turned the telescope around and said, 'Here, chum. Try it this way.' I did. And wow!"

In *From Striving to Thriving: How to Grow Confident, Capable Readers* (2017), Annie and Steph write, "Watershed reading experiences are the catalysts that transform many readers from striving to thriving."

Set Expectations and Measure Reading Volume

Volume, yes. But how much reading is enough? In her role as elementary literacy ambassador, Maggie frequently finds herself advocating for reading volume with colleagues, who inevitably ask her for a definition of reading volume and quantifiable targets. To answer their question, as well as to satisfy her own curiosity, Maggie began with the writing of Reading Hall of Famer Richard Allington: "Reading volume is defined as the combination of time students spend reading plus the number of words they actually consume as they read" (2012).

Because Allington's definition focuses on rate, Maggie focused there. If you asked any Mamaroneck educator how much time we expect children to spend reading each day, she would say a minimum of 60 minutes: 20+ minutes during reading workshop, 10+ additional minutes at other points in the school day, and 30+ minutes at home. Assuming 60 minutes of reading time per day, then, how much volume should children accrue each day or across a week? To answer that question, Maggie turned to a massive study completed by Hasbrouck and Tindal (2017). The researchers gathered data on children's reading rates in grades 1 to 8 in fall, winter, and spring, in a range of proficiency percentile levels (e.g., 10th, 25th, 50th, 75th, 90th).

HOW MUCH VOLUME SHOULD STRIVING READERS ACCRUE WITH 60 MINUTES OF READING PER DAY?

WINTER OF GRADE	SAMPLE TITLE	AVERAGE WINTER FLUENCY FOR STRIVING READERS	LEVEL	WORDS IN THE SAMPLE TITLE	APPROX. TIME	APPROXIMATE NUMBER OF BOOKS (assuming 60 min. of daily reading)
1	The Lost Bear	In the winter of first grade, a striving reader in the 25th percentile reads on average **16 words per minute**	D	134	8 minutes	**7.5 books per day**
2	Don't Worry, BEE Happy	In the winter of second grade, a striving reader in the 25th percentile reads on average **59 words per minute**	H	342	6 minutes	**10 books per day**
3	THE INFAMOUS RATSOS	In the winter of third grade, a striving reader in the 25th percentile reads on average **79 words per minute**	L	2,422	30 minutes	**2 books per day**
4	DYAMONDE DANIEL RICH	In the winter of fourth grade, a striving reader in the 25th percentile reads on average **95 words per minute**	Q	5,217	60 minutes	**1 book per day**
5	JAKE MADDOX SOCCER STAND-OFF	In the winter of fifth grade, a striving reader in the 25th percentile reads on average **109 words per minute**	R	11,353	100 minutes	**3 books per week** (Monday–Friday)

Hasbrouck & Tindal, 2017 (eric.ed.gov/?id=ED605146)

Using the rates in the study and the running word counts of familiar books, Maggie calculated approximately how long it should take readers to finish books at their independent reading level. For example, *The Infamous Ratsos* has 2,422 words. At 79 words per minute, it should take a striving third grader about 30 minutes to read it, allowing plenty of time to get started on the next book in the series. Maggie was stunned because she regularly saw children spend many days reading a single Infamous Ratsos book. Even allowing for normal pauses (e.g., to stop and think, share a compelling passage), a striving reader should be able to make his way through several Infamous Ratsos books over the course of a week.

Maggie proceeded to study 30 to 40 other books across grade levels, seeking to determine how many of them children should read over the course of a day or week, when given 60 minutes of reading time per day. In each case, she reached the same astonishing conclusion: striving readers were falling woefully short of volume!

Furthermore, when Maggie performed a similar analysis using the rates of children reading in the 50th percentile, she concluded that even these seemingly proficient readers were in danger of slipping because they were evidently reading far less than the 60 minutes per day prescribed by the district for reading in school and at home. What was going on? Was it possible that…

- children who weren't well-matched with books were distracted during independent reading time (e.g., chatting, taking bathroom breaks)?
- long mini-lessons ("maxi-lessons") and accountability measures such as reading responses and exit tickets were encroaching on independent reading time?
- pull-out intervention lessons were supplanting rather than supplementing children's independent reading time?

To uphold expectations for reading volume, the Mamaroneck team set out to track the amount of actual reading each child did across a day, week, month, and year. Maggie and Suzanne developed the Volume Tracker, described on page 70, began to use it with students, and incorporated it into an in-service course they were facilitating for district teachers. (See Volume + Capability on the next page.)

Teachers in the course were taken aback by the information Maggie and Suzanne presented and set out to teach their students about reading volume: what it is, why it matters so much, and how to increase it. (See "Teach the Importance of Volume" on page 162.) Third-grade teacher Jennifer Solomon reported that her students took the information to heart and set more ambitious volume goals for themselves. They prioritized independent reading at home and kept track of pages read each day, noting at the end of each week whether they had met or fallen short of their goals—and why. "Kids are becoming more invested in their independent reading," Jennifer noted in a course reflection. "They speak knowledgeably about their goals, what gets in their way, and how they plan to overcome hurdles."

A NOTE ON VOLUME TARGETS

In Mamaroneck we have stopped short of setting a specific page count or book count for each grade level. Instead, we have adopted a multi-year stretch goal to ensure that all children read capably and voluminously across genres for a variety of authentic and meaningful purposes, and leave it to teachers to follow the guidelines in this chapter to promote voluminous reading. In our experience, numerical targets lead to an unproductive focus on book length that sometimes dissuades students from selecting longer books.

VOLUME + CAPABILITY

While comparing notes on their coaching in Mamaroneck, Maggie and Suzanne noticed a pattern. Teachers in grades 3–5 were eager to learn effective strategies for supporting children with decoding and encoding at the word level. Although Mamaroneck has long had a robust phonics program in the primary grades, teachers were finding that some children continued to need support with phonics concepts and spelling as they made their way to third grade and beyond. Maggie and Suzanne saw this as an opportunity to help teachers integrate capability-based instruction (e.g., targeted phonics lessons, comprehension strategies) with volume-based interventions. In response, they designed an intensive, six-session in-service course called Reading Volume + Capability.

The course begins with a close look at the virtuous cycle and a rich discussion of how reading volume and reading capability work in tandem to propel readers forward. Each participating teacher selects a striving reader with gaps in phonics knowledge and sets to work establishing a robust reading life, in which the child accrues vital reading volume using the techniques described in Parts II and III of this book. The group then learns how to pinpoint specific areas of need at the word level (e.g., vowel digraphs, syllabication) and how to provide quick, explicit, and targeted instruction to meet the child's specific phonics needs. At the end of each lesson, children return to their independent reading books to put into practice the skills they worked on in isolation. As this phonics instruction progresses across weeks or months, teachers continue to monitor and support students' reading volume. Tara's gains are among many success stories from this professional development experience.

Respect and Track All Forms of Engaged Reading

Readers sometimes blaze through books—particularly series books, as Tara did—consuming them in a linear, rapid, and continuous stream. This volume is evident and relatively easy to quantify. And readers also spend time poring over books they treasure, such as meaty, non-narrative nonfiction—reading and rereading them, studying text features, gleaning information, inferring, and pondering, as fifth grader Michael is doing in the photo below with *The Super Human Encyclopedia*.

As volume-building efforts have taken root in Mamaroneck, we have grappled with how to honor and record the various ways successful readers spend their time in books, particularly the high-interest books in formats and genres we have worked so hard to add to classroom library collections, such as cookbooks, atlases, "compendia" of fascinating facts, joke books, and graphic novels.

This form of reading volume—characterized by rapt enthrallment, but fewer page turns—is more difficult to quantify, yet we know it leads to reading gains. This recognition, coupled with Steph's enormous and rightful emphasis on the power of nonfiction to hook readers,

Michael reading *The Super Human Encyclopedia*

leads us to augment Allington's definition. In addition to the number of words children consume as they read, we kidwatch for other indicators of voluminous high-success reading experiences. A child is likely having a voluminous, high-success reading experience if he or she does the following:

- Keeps a book close at hand
- Reads voluntarily (i.e., without prompting); takes advantage of free bits of time to read, as the enthralled middle schooler pictured below does on her way from class to class
- Progresses through a book at full steam *or* lingers in the book, captivated
- Radiates enthusiasm about a book: talks about it, shares snippets, recommends it, takes action in response to it (see Diagnostic Question 4 on page 89)
- Springboards from one book to others (e.g., the next books in the series, other books on the same compelling topic)

When this reader finally got her hands on a coveted copy of *Rebound* by Kwame Alexander, she literally couldn't put it down!

Ed Urso, teacher of Michael (pictured on the previous page), recognized Michael's ardent interest in human body systems and the amount of time he spent reading and rereading *The Super Human Encyclopedia*. Not surprisingly, Michael chose to focus on the circulatory system for his fifth- grade Capstone Project and took delight in recounting the fascinating facts he was learning. (*Did you know that the circulatory system contains 60,000+ miles of blood vessels, enough to encircle the globe more than twice?*) Noticing that Michael was reading only informational text during independent reading during the weeks of Capstone Project, Ed took care to confer with him about the whole-class read-aloud of *Tuck Everlasting* to make sure that Michael was also developing the ability to analyze character and other literary elements, which he wasn't encountering in his informational text reading.

While visiting a seventh-grade math class, Annie noted with interest that several children took out their independent reading books after completing math "exit tickets" in the final two minutes of class. Whereas many tweens would run down the clock until the bell rang, these kids seized the opportunity to dive back into their books. When Annie conferred with one of them, Johnny, he confirmed that he "couldn't wait to find out what happened" in his graphic novel and that he "wanted to look at the page again" to make sure he had inferred correctly what had transpired between frames. Rather than worry that Johnny was processing less text than a peer reading a traditional novel, Annie recognized Johnny's unprompted reach for the book and engagement as signs of high-success reading.

When tracking children's reading journeys, be on alert for signs of growth, enthusiasm, agency, confidence, and reading identity—indicators of the virtuous cycle.

Having emphasized the power of children entering the virtuous cycle, we turn our attention in Chapter 2 to the foundational actions you can take across the year to create the conditions in which voluminous, high-success reading isn't merely possible, but rather inevitable.

Voluminous Reading: Nine Foundational Actions

Third-grade teacher Lorraine Leddy reached into a classroom library bin and retrieved several books for a Getting-to-Know-You Preview Stack (see page 111). New to Mamaroneck, Lorraine was eager to assess her students using the technique from the district's assessment framework. She planned to confer early with Brianna, a striving reader, to get her up and running in a compelling book and to learn about her reading history and preferences. Lorraine found that the classroom library she inherited contained few books at Brianna's last assessed reading level—specifically, four Henry and Mudge books from 2005—even though the collection filled several bookcases. Lorraine thought about the message the classroom library would send to Brianna. If the books in it were worn and limited, would she assume they were her only choice? Likely, she would.

Lorraine knew that her personal children's book collection, while extensive, would not fill the gap. She recognized the need to weed, inventory, and augment the classroom library, and reached out to Maggie for support. Maggie was not surprised to hear from Lorraine, having already anticipated the collection would need attention due to teacher turnover. Two of Maggie's primary roles as literacy ambassador are to ensure that every classroom is outfitted with a serviceable library and to support every teacher in augmenting and customizing it across the year with a district budget allocation. In the Mamaroneck team's experience, collections erode when teachers are reassigned or retire. Books migrate from one classroom to another, often leaving behind motley collections mismatched to readers—particularly strivers, as Lorraine found.

Maggie helped Lorraine conduct an inventory, using a free online electronic management tool. Using two portable scanners, Maggie, Lorraine, and two student volunteers managed to scan 75 percent of the books in the collection in a single lunch period. Later, Maggie scanned the remaining books and compiled a spreadsheet of over 600 titles, organized by text level. Maggie also created charts, like the one on the next page, so Lorraine could see the overall distribution of text levels in the collection, as well as the distribution of levels recommended for third-grade libraries, Levels K–P, in green.

Lorraine noted that the collection skewed high, a pattern Maggie had found in many classroom libraries in the district prior to curation. A substantial number of books were at Levels P–Z, well beyond the year-end benchmark for third grade: Level O. With Brianna in mind,

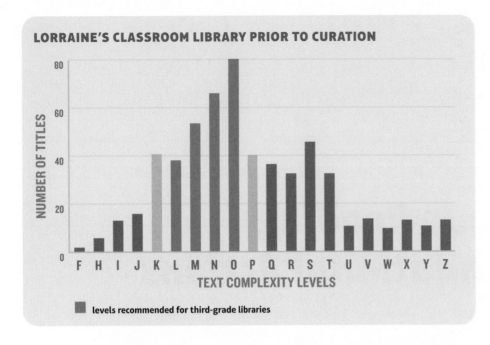

LORRAINE'S CLASSROOM LIBRARY PRIOR TO CURATION

NUMBER OF TITLES

TEXT COMPLEXITY LEVELS

F H I J K L M N O P Q R S T U V W X Y Z

■ levels recommended for third-grade libraries

Lorraine was shocked to find that her library originally contained more Level S books than Levels F–J books combined!

Lorraine started by moving most of the books at Level Q and higher to storage bins, immediately thinning the collection to better match the readers in the room. "Students were more likely to encounter books that would ensure successful, joyful reading experiences," Lorraine commented. She redistributed some of the books she'd removed to fourth- and fifth- grade teachers; others she held in reserve for mini-lessons, read-alouds, and more developed readers' independent reading.

Once the library contained a majority of books appropriate for third grade, gaps became evident in, for example, nonfiction and fantasy fiction. Lorraine noted a dearth of books by and about BIPOC individuals and people with disabilities. Armed with this information, she set out to acquire high-quality books by diverse authors that spanned a range of genres, formats, and topics. (See #ownvoices later in this chapter.) Maggie gave Lorraine a baseline list of books she'd ordered for past "infusions" into third-grade classroom libraries, and Lorraine asked her students for book recommendations.

Lorraine circled back to Brianna with a robust Preview Stack containing fiction and nonfiction books, in graphic format and standard chapter book format, on topics such as sports, friendship, space exploration, animals, and cooking. "Watching Brianna interact with a new-and-improved Preview Stack gave me such a vivid understanding of her reading life, as well as her personality," Lorraine commented. "I learned so much about her interests, thanks to the variety of books I made available to her." For example, when presented with a biography from the Little People, BIG DREAMS series, Brianna told Lorraine she loves stories about real people. An animal lover, Brianna also leaned into a book from the Who's a Good Dog? series. With a steady stream of appealing books—and Lorraine's support—Brianna made great strides throughout the year.

Change the book, change the reader! Chances are, when students lack confidence and motivation to read, it's because key elements that assure high-success reading are not yet in place. Time for a gut check! Have you ensured that all your students:

- Have access to books they can and want to read?
- Are given daily uninterrupted time to read?
- Are part of a classroom reading culture that encourages and supports their voluminous reading every day?

By embracing the following actions, you'll create optimal conditions for independent reading for every child, and you'll answer "yes" to those three critical questions.

Nine Actions That Promote Voluminous Reading

By thoughtfully curating her classroom library, Lorraine created conditions for striving reader Brianna to thrive. She also set up the rest of her class to read successfully and independently. In Part II, which provides the tools to support individual readers intensively, you'll notice that we periodically redirect you back to this chapter to make sure you're embracing critical, foundational actions. When you do, you equip most kids to read voluminously, which enables you to focus your volume-building attention on those kids who need it most.

Know Kids in the Round

Because children thrive when they feel known and valued, building genuine and trusting relationships is the core of our work. In a profound essay in *The Teacher You Want to Be*, Katherine Bomer urges that we view students "with an air of expectancy," taking an open, inquisitive, and appreciative stance as we get to know them over time: "Notice that the actions of looking, listening, and accepting require us to change our stance in the classroom from being the constant deliverer of information, source of all answers, and evaluator and judge...to becoming curious, empathetic, and accepting of what is in our students" (2015).

The following prompts help you get to know each of your students and focus your teaching accordingly. For example, from informal conversations, Lorraine knew that Brianna had two older brothers at home who were thriving readers of chapter books. From queries from Brianna's mother, she knew that there was interest in advancing Brianna to chapter books as well. Lorraine put that knowledge to use in two ways: 1. She assured Brianna's parents that the Little People, BIG DREAMS biographies Brianna was reading were appropriately meaty. 2. She suspected that Brianna would seek hefty books to keep up with her brothers and classmates, and would need to find thick yet accessible anthologies to fit the bill.

Know a Child as a Person

- Who are the important people in his life? What are their occupations, schedules, and preferred modes of communication?
- Are other language(s) spoken at home?
- What are the child's interests? What does he know and care a lot about? Does he play a sport, belong to a club, or pursue a hobby?
- What responsibilities (chores, sibling care, job) does he have beyond schoolwork?
- Who are his friends?

Know a Child as a Learner

- What have his prior school experiences been like?
- What curricular topics interest him most? Least?
- Does he prefer to collaborate or work independently?
- Does he have reliable access to tech tools and the Internet outside of school?
- What is his level of academic self-confidence?

Know a Child as a Reader

- What is the child's reading history (textual lineage)? What landmark texts and reading experiences has he had?
- What are his literary tastes and preferences? What kinds of reading does he gravitate toward? Avoid?
- What experience has he had navigating different genres and formats?
- What meaning-making strategies does he use independently?
- How does the child see himself as a reader?
- What access streams does the child have? How many books are available at home? Does he use school and public libraries?
- Is he in a book club or partnership?
- Are there expectations or restrictions from parents about what the child reads?

Ways to Know a Child in the Round

- Kidwatch: Observe the child, noting his behaviors, interactions, response to challenges.
- Confer: Meet with the child individually; ask him about prior experiences, perceptions of himself as a learner and reader.
- Chat with the child before/after class, at lunch; find out what's on his mind.
- Converse with parents or caregivers: seek and share perspectives about the child.
- Study the student's work carefully, not just to assess its completeness and accuracy but to see what it reveals about his thinking and study habits.
- Inventory the child's interests, background knowledge, and preferences.
- Invite parents to provide information about the child via a parent input form.
- Use diagnostic assessments (e.g., Getting-to-Know-You Preview Stack, page 111) to assess the child's prior experiences and preferences.
- Consult with other professionals who know the child well, such as prior teachers and counselors.
- Make a home visit: Visit the child and his family at home in a relaxed, informal manner. See page 168 for more information on home visits.

Knowing children as people, learners, and readers—really knowing them—builds productive, trusting relationships and guides our teaching. Just as the best gift givers use what they know about friends and family to choose thoughtful gifts, teachers who use what they know about their students design innovative, literacy-boosting strategies tailored to kids' needs, as we'll discuss in Chapter 3. Knowing kids as people first leads us to understand them better as readers.

2 Book-Match Relentlessly

With deep gratitude to Teri Lesesne (2003), educator and book maven extraordinaire, we recognize that "making the match" between reader and book—and protecting the flame once it's lit—is a vital responsibility for anyone who champions children's literacy development. We use the word "relentlessly" because our commitment must be steady and ongoing. We serve as keepers of the flame when we focus on the dynamics between individual readers and their books. When we express genuine interest in their book choices, children sense it; they know we mean it when we say we want them to be enthralled by what they read. At first, they meet us halfway by offering honest opinions about our recommendations; eventually, they become active and agentive seekers of texts they want to read.

Here are our suggestions for making great book-matches for your readers.

- **Notice the physical relationship between children and their books.** Engaged readers keep their books close at hand and open them whenever they have a free moment. Although it sounds obvious, one of the first signs that a reader is not well matched with a book is, well, the absence of that book! For example, when Annie asked fifth grader Elvis what he was reading, he plunged his hand deep into his desk and retrieved two empty Doritos bags before a tattered paperback. He looked at the book (presumably to remind himself of its title) before holding it up for approval.

- **Inquire into children's book choices.** When kids do appear to be suitably matched, ask them about the book they've chosen. Where did they find it? What about it appealed to them? How have they made their way into it? Questions like those help you gauge the child's level of investment in the book and identify the book-access streams they tap (e.g., home, public and school libraries). We have found that while thriving readers generally have multiple streams, striving readers often rely solely on classroom libraries and collections in literacy-support settings if they receive in-services outside the classroom, making it all the more important that those streams contain a wealth of highly accessible and appealing books (see Action 3 on page 29). And if a child like Elvis is not invested in his book, we ought to pause and help him reconsider his selection before tying instruction or accountability measures to a book he cares little about. We spend a great deal of time conferring with children about their book choices and selection processes.

- **Model ways you plan for and conduct your reading life.** Let kids know how finicky you are about what you read. ("So many books, so little time.") Show them how you identify potential Next-Up books by reading reviews, seeking recommendations from readers with similar tastes to yours, browsing libraries and bookstores, and reading the flaps and opening pages of potential books. Point out that once you've started reading a book, you keep it with you to maintain momentum; you read during downtime in waiting rooms, on the train, and so forth. Explain that when you let too much time elapse without reading, you can have trouble re-entering the world of the book.

- **Use Preview Stacks to assess kids' preferences and match them with compelling books.** We have found Donalyn Miller's book-matching technique to be so effective that we have incorporated a variation, a Getting-to-Know-You Preview Stack, into our elementary assessment framework at the outset of the year. In the conference, the child sorts a set of books you've assembled by preference, and you learn the genres, formats, designs, and other elements that appeal to—or repel—her. At the end of the conference, ideally, the child leaves with one or more good matches, and you leave with valuable assessment data to guide your recommendations going forward. (See details on Getting-to-Know-You Preview Stacks on page 111.)

- **Avoid book snobbery:** Do you look askance at funny/edgy topics and graphic formats and frown upon rereading? To be effective book-matchers, we must instead allow kids to choose and delight in books of all stripes, including graphic novels and book adaptations of movies and TV shows. As Jeffrey Wilhelm, Michael Smith, and Sharon Fransen suggest in *Reading Unbound: Why Kids Need to Read What They Want and Why We Should Let Them* (2013), we must ask, "If we want to develop engaged and competent readers, might we not benefit from understanding the nature of reading pleasure, particularly in relation to the books that students love, but that we, as adults and teachers, might disapprove of?"

  In Mamaroneck, when we looked at the school library circulation data of children who'd made accelerated gains as readers, we noticed a clear and fascinating pattern of rereading! Rather than signifying reading "ruts," repeated checkouts point to engaged reading spurts, as captured in Maisie's circulation record, shown below. She checked out *High School Musical* seven times in two months!

- **Guide students to keep Next-Up Book List.** A Next-Up Book List (or "books on deck") is a simple volume-building tool that prevents stalls and gaps in kids' reading lives and gives you a window into their intentions. Prompt students to keep a running list in their reading notebooks or folders of appealing titles they've heard about from one another, your booktalks, or other sources. Look at those lists regularly to make sure kids have Next-Up books in mind while they're still devouring their current one. Step in to procure Next-Up books for children who lack access. (To learn more about Next-Up Book Lists, see page 121.)

- **Guide and track readers' paths.** Next-Up Book Lists can also serve as reading logs if students record the books they have read, as well as books they plan to read. Encourage kids to use their lists to reflect on their reading paths, noticing whether and how their preferences are evolving. On page 125, read more about Teri Lesesne's concept of "reading ladders" (2010) as a way to support a reader's progress from book to book.

Big Nate : In a Class by Himself (Copy: T 52448)	5/19/2015	5/25/2015	5/29/2015
Little Miss Sunshine and the wicked witch (Copy Deleted: T 52350)	5/11/2015	5/18/2015	5/19/2015
Little Miss Splendid and the princess (Copy Deleted: T 52349)	5/11/2015	5/18/2015	5/19/2015
High school musical : the essential guide (Copy Deleted: T 51417)	5/1/2015	5/7/2015	5/11/2015
High school musical : the essential guide (Copy Deleted: T 51417)	4/15/2015	4/21/2015	5/1/2015
Japan : a question and answer book (Copy: T 127802)	4/15/2015	4/21/2015	6/15/2015
Japan (Copy: T 51643)	4/15/2015	4/21/2015	6/15/2015
High school musical : the essential guide (Copy Deleted: T 51417)	4/7/2015	4/13/2015	4/15/2015
Kim Possible. Volume 6 (Copy: T 50866)	4/7/2015	4/13/2015	4/15/2015
Kim Possible. Volume 6 (Copy: T 50866)	3/23/2015	3/30/2015	4/7/2015
High school musical : the essential guide (Copy Deleted: T 51417)	3/23/2015	3/30/2015	4/7/2015
High school musical : the essential guide (Copy Deleted: T 51417)	3/13/2015	3/19/2015	3/23/2015
Kim Possible. Volume 6 (Copy: T 50866)	3/13/2015	3/19/2015	3/23/2015
Kim Possible. Volume 6 (Copy: T 50866)	3/4/2015	3/10/2015	3/13/2015
High school musical : the essential guide (Copy Deleted: T 51417)	3/4/2015	3/10/2015	3/13/2015
Kim Possible. Volume 7 (Copy: T 50867)	2/24/2015	3/2/2015	3/4/2015
High school musical : the essential guide (Copy Deleted: T 51417)	2/24/2015	3/2/2015	3/4/2015
Romeo & Juliet (Copy: T 52602)	1/30/2015	2/5/2015	2/9/2015
Kim Possible. Volume 1 (Copy: T 127771)	1/30/2015	2/5/2015	1/30/2015
Kim Possible. Volume 7 (Copy: T 50867)	1/30/2015	2/5/2015	2/24/2015

Maisie's library circulation history

3 Create and Curate Robust, Vibrant, and Diverse Classroom Libraries

Access to books is a social justice issue. Classroom libraries provide children with fingertip access to appealing texts to read voluminously. That access is essential for all children, especially for striving readers and children in poverty, for whom the classroom library is likely the most reliable source of books. Equity and access go together. School needs to be the place kids can find and read the books they love.

Like planting a garden, curating a collection takes active, ongoing attention. Once we make the powerful decision to support all our readers with a classroom library, we must commit to curating the collection. In making an argument for increased book allocations for district-wide classroom libraries, Annie explained to the Board of Education that Mamaroneck teachers are in the business of facilitating 5,600 unique and idiosyncratic reading journeys! It takes time, energy, and resources to build and maintain the classroom libraries each of our children needs.

- **Take stock of what you've inherited, and weed aggressively.** Less is indeed more! While it may seem counterintuitive to cull your collection as a first step in building it, we can't emphasize enough that fewer but appealing high-quality books are far more valuable than a sprawling collection of unappealing, dated ones. In fact, we've found that library circulation typically increases following substantial weeding because readers are able to locate and peruse books more easily.

  Involve students in weeding. In our experience, they will have few qualms about identifying books they won't read!

- **Build the collection for the readers you expect.** Over time, aim to acquire a core collection of books well suited to the capabilities and interests of most children at your grade level. That means familiarizing yourself with tried-and-true topics, authors, and series, as well as actively and continuously seeking new ones. As you do so, keep the following criteria in mind.

  - ▶ **Variety and appeal:** Select books in a wide range of formats, genres, and topics. Be aware of your own tastes and preferences, and make sure you acquire books well beyond them. For example, when Annie was an eighth-grade English teacher, her classroom library was low on two of her least favorite genres, fantasy fiction and science fiction, until her students brought those gaps to her attention. In our frequent tours of classrooms, we notice that collections often fall short on books that are funny, edgy, "forbidden," or inspired by pop culture—the very things that appeal to young readers.

  - ▶ **Effort-to-reward ratio:** Consider books' "effort-to-reward ratios." Striving readers benefit from books that provide multiple entry points and immediate gratification, such as graphic novels and image-heavy formats. Make sure your library includes books that require less effort from the reader to achieve high levels of satisfaction.

  - ▶ **Text quality:** Turn to reliable sources and advocacy groups, such as The Conscious Kid and We Need Diverse Books, to inform your choices for fiction and nonfiction. (See the resources in Decolonizing Our Bookshelves, page 32.)

Students in Janet Acobes's third-grade class relished her invitation to pull dated books out of the classroom library.

- **An appropriate range of levels:** *From Striving to Thriving: How to Grow Confident, Capable Readers* (2017) contains the eye-opening results of a room-by-room inventory of classroom libraries in Mamaroneck, revealing that, prior to any systemic attention, the vast majority of those libraries skewed high. In fact, most collections—including the one Lorraine inherited—contained mostly books that were at higher levels than district year-end benchmarks demanded! By favoring the already-thriving readers, this mismatch exacerbated the Matthew effects we describe in Chapter 1 and left many strivers in de facto book droughts.

- **Customize the collection for the readers you meet,** using what you know about kids' interests to acquire high-interest topics, formats, and genres. Stock and renew the shelves, keeping these points in mind:

  ▸ **Kid recommendations:** Tap all your readers, especially strivers. Anticipate high-interest tie-ins for movies and TV shows (e.g., books based on animated favorites such as *Frozen* and *Coco*). These high-currency titles provide big bang for the buck, even if they self-destruct after repeated, joyful readings. McGill-Franzen and Allington (2010) found that books featuring pop-culture personalities and characters (e.g., Lil' Romeo, Britney Spears, Pokemon, Captain Underpants) were the most highly sought titles by children in their summer slide prevention study.

A NOTE ON TEXT LEVELS

We advocate for paying attention to text levels but strongly believe those levels are a teacher's tool, not a child's label! (Parrott, 2017) Paying professional attention to levels behind the scenes enables us to de-emphasize levels when conferring with students, because it ensures the bulk of the collection is well suited to the majority of them.

CUSTOMIZE THE COLLECTION FOR THE READERS YOU MEET

Second-grade teacher Arelys Vieira used her district allocation to purchase books featuring characters from *Frozen* and *Moana* at the peak of their popularity and to beef up her collection of sports-trivia books, based on student demand. Noticing that several kids were aspiring master chefs, she also fed the class's interest with cookbooks.

► **Niche acquisitions:** If you receive an allocation from your school or district, use it to purchase books that match students' assessed interests, particularly striving readers'. For example, as fourth-grader Layna was considering books Maggie offered in a Preview Stack, she rejected a how-to book on hairstyling but acknowledged that she would be interested in a how-to book on skateboarding. In other words, she was intrigued by Maggie's choice of format, but not of topic. So Maggie found a how-to book on skateboarding and ordered it for Layna, knowing that it would likely jump-start her reading.

► **Seasonal, timely satellite collections:** Borrowing books from school and public libraries is a no-cost way of augmenting your collection to match students' passing interests. For example, in Olympics years, kids love reading about the Games: their history, popular and lesser-known sports, and medal-winning athletes. Also, coffee (or "cocoa") table books are expensive to purchase but can be borrowed from the library for a rotating, high-interest classroom center.

► **Access to other libraries' collections:** Partner with school and public librarians to increase your students' access to high-interest titles. Once you've stoked demand for specific books through booktalks and read-alouds, you'll likely need to supply multiple copies to eager readers. Librarians can help you round up books through interlibrary loan so that kids can read and discuss them simultaneously, fueling social energy in your classroom.

● **Establish an ongoing cycle of weeding and expansion:** Following the initial weeding described above, periodically throughout the year remove dated and/or worn books from your collection and acquire new ones. Keep an ongoing "wish list" of titles you'd like to add. If you do not receive a book allocation—or if your school's purchasing procedures are cumbersome, speak with the appropriate administrator about the cost-effectiveness of targeted book-matching as a volume-building strategy. Share the essay entitled "Riverkeepers: Strategies to Keep Vital Streams of Books Flowing," contributed by Annie and Maggie to *Game Changer! Book Access for All Kids* (2018), which you can find at scholastic.com/ReinventionResources.

Tracking the Representation of People of Color in Children's Literature

- In a 1965 *Saturday Review* article, "The All-White World of Children's Books," Dr. Nancy Larrick, founder of the International Literacy Association, contrasts population data with children's book publishing statistics, and exposes a vast overrepresentation of white characters: "Integration may be the law of the land, but most of the books children see are all white." This dearth harms children of color by depriving them of opportunities to see themselves in the books they read and in how they imagine their futures. It also harms white children. As Larrick puts it, "Although his light skin makes him one of the world's minorities, the white child learns from his books that he is the kingfish. There seems to be little chance of developing the humility so needed for world cooperation."

- Almost 50 years later, in response to a 2013 study by the Cooperative Children's Book Center at the University of Wisconsin, author Walter Dean Myers (2014) published an op-ed piece in *The New York Times*, "Where Are the People of Color in Children's Books?," decrying the persistent problem. Myers describes his own path to literacy, including his adolescent disenchantment with reading because he didn't see himself or others like him in books: "As I discovered who I was, a black teenager in a white-dominated world, I saw that these characters, these lives, were not mine. I didn't want to become the 'black representative,' or some shining example of diversity. What I wanted, needed really, was to become an integral and valued part of the mosaic that I saw around me."

- Alongside that piece, author Christopher Myers (2014), son of Walter Dean Myers, published an op-ed titled "The Apartheid of Children's Literature," in which he posits that for children of color, books function as maps: "[Children of color] are indeed searching for their place in the world, but they are also deciding where they want to go. They create, through the stories they're given, an atlas of their world, of their relationships to others, of their possible destinations." Citing the scarcity of books about and featuring people of color, Myers concludes, "Children of color remain outside the boundaries of imagination. The cartography we create with this literature is flawed."

- In 2016 and again in 2019, Dr. Sarah Park Dahlen, associate professor in the Master of Library and Information Science Program at St. Catherine University, and Minnesota illustrator David Huyck published an infographic depicting data collected by the Cooperative Children's Book Center at University of Wisconsin—M adison, about books published in those years depicting characters from diverse backgrounds. Staggeringly, the statistics reveal minimal progress had been made in half a century. Whereas 50 percent of the books published featured white characters and 27 percent featured animals and other nonhuman characters, only 1 percent featured American Indians, 5 percent featured Latinx people, 7 percent featured Asian-Pacific Islanders or Asian-Pacific Americans, and 10 percent featured Africans or African Americans. Note Huyck's depiction of the small, warped, and/or broken mirrors held by characters of color in comparison to the myriad, favorable reflections of the white character, who is privileged to see himself from all angles as royalty, space traveler, athlete, and more.

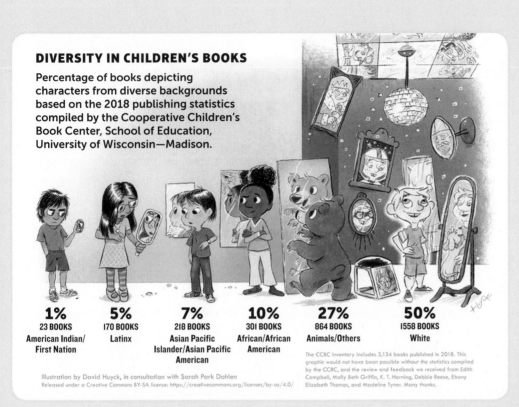

DIVERSITY IN CHILDREN'S BOOKS

Percentage of books depicting characters from diverse backgrounds based on the 2018 publishing statistics compiled by the Cooperative Children's Book Center, School of Education, University of Wisconsin—Madison.

1%
23 BOOKS
American Indian/
First Nation

5%
170 BOOKS
Latinx

7%
218 BOOKS
Asian Pacific
Islander/Asian Pacific
American

10%
301 BOOKS
African/African
American

27%
864 BOOKS
Animals/Others

50%
1558 BOOKS
White

The CCBC inventory includes 3,134 books published in 2018. This graphic would not have been possible without the statistics compiled by the CCBC, and the review and feedback we received from Edith Campbell, Molly Beth Griffin, K. T. Horning, Debbie Reese, Ebony Elizabeth Thomas, and Madeline Tyner. Many thanks.

- In a follow-up blog post (2019), Dr. Dahlen explains that she and Huyck "wanted this infographic to show not just the low quantity of existing literature, but also the inaccuracy and uneven quality of some of those books," particularly those not written in #OwnVoices.

- In February 2020, educator and author Zaretta Hammond contributed a piece to the Research for Better Teaching's newsletter, "Revisiting Your Library: Decolonizing, Not Just Diversifying." Hammond argues that building a diverse collection is insufficient: "We add books with more brown faces, but we may still be perpetuating stereotypes." For example, Hammond states that many so-called "diverse" books feature Black people in predictable roles. "Most often, they are about buses, boycotts, or basketball. They are storylines that are often about the challenges of 'urban or inner-city' living. Or those books center around a 'Black Lives Matter' social justice theme, depict African Americans during slavery or the civil rights era, focusing on 'heroes and holidays.' Lastly, a common stereotypical theme is Black kids and sports as a way to increase reading engagement, especially among boys." Hammond emphasizes that those types of books have a place in a well-curated collection, but they should not rule. "In reality, Black life is diverse. The Black experience is diverse. Our classroom libraries should reflect that reality, too." Hammond offers three questions to assess whether a book is worth including or not:

    1. Does the book go beyond typical themes about characters of color?

    2. Do the children of color look authentic?

    3. Are the texts, especially fictional stories, "enabling"?

Echoing Nancy Larrick's point from a half-century ago, Hammond concludes that those questions will help educators identify books that affirm African American students and "expand white students' exposure to the everydayness of Black life in America and around the world."

Viewing Books as Mirrors, Windows, Sliding Glass Doors... and Prisms

Few literary metaphors have been as apt, provocative, and lasting as ones coined by Rudine Sims Bishop in an essay in which she explains how books can serve as "mirrors," "windows," and "sliding glass doors" for readers:

> "Books are sometimes windows, offering views of worlds that may be real or imagined, familiar or strange. These windows are also sliding glass doors, and readers have only to walk through in imagination to become part of whatever world has been created and recreated by the author. When lighting conditions are just right, however, a window can also be a mirror. Literature transforms human experience and reflects it back to us, and in that reflection we can see our own lives and experiences as part of the larger human experience. Reading, then, becomes a means of self-affirmation, and readers often seek their mirrors in books" (1990).

Those metaphors are apt to readers who have been jolted by seeing their own experiences reflected on the page or who have traveled beyond those experiences, thanks to a book. They are provocative because Bishop states plainly that nonwhite readers, too often, come up empty when they search for mirrors: "When children cannot find themselves reflected in the books they read, or when the images they see are distorted, negative, or laughable, they learn a powerful lesson about how they are devalued in the society of which they are a part." Finally, the metaphors are lasting because they have been cited innumerable times over the last 30 years—albeit often without attribution.

In an article in *The Horn Book Magazine* (2019), children's author Uma Krishnaswami revisits Bishop's metaphors and asks, Why stop with windows and mirrors? She reviews several children's books and suggests that they operate as prisms, shedding new light on readers' lives and perspectives:

> "A prism can slow and bend the light that passes through it, splitting that light into its component colors. It can refract light in as many directions as the prism's shape and surface planes allow. Similarly, books can disrupt and challenge ideas about diversity through multifaceted and intersecting identities, settings, cultural contexts, and histories. They can place diverse characters at these crucial intersections and give them the power to reframe their stories. Through the fictional world, they can make us question the assumptions and practices of our own real world."

Resources

Follow these individuals, organizations, and hashtags for current, reliable information to bring diverse and authentic texts to your students.

AMERICAN INDIANS IN CHILDREN'S LITERATURE (AICL)

americanindiansinchildrensliterature.net

Established in 2006 by Dr. Debbie Reese of Nambé Pueblo, American Indians in Children's Literature (AICL) provides critical analysis of indigenous peoples in children's and young adult books. Dr. Jean Mendoza is a co-editor at AICL.

Dr. Debbie Reese is on Twitter @debreese

EDITH (EDI) CAMPBELL

crazyquiltedi.blog

Edi Campbell is a reference/instruction librarian at Indiana State University committed to improving the representation of people of color and native/First Nations People in children's literature by addressing issues of bias, racism, inequity, and imperialism. An avid quilter, Campbell named her blog CrazyQuiltEdi, noting: "Crazy quilts are a unique type of quilt that combines fabrics of all shapes, sizes, textures, and colors into a unique piece of art.... When 'scraps' come together, they create a thing of beauty."

Edi Campbell is on Twitter @crazyquilts

COOPERATIVE CENTER FOR CHILDREN'S BOOKS

ccbc.education.wisc.edu

Established in 1963, the CCBC is a unique research library at the University of Wisconsin—Madison, School of Education. Its mission is to identify outstanding children's literature and bring it to the attention of educators and others interested in connecting children with great books. Director Kathleen T. Horning and librarians Merry Lindgren, Megan Schliesman, and Madeline Tyner post trustworthy resources, including Book of the Week reviews (archived from 1997) and an array of awards and best-of-the-year lists, as well as a detailed multicultural literature resource.

CCBC Librarians are on Twitter @ccbcwisc

THE CONSCIOUS KID

theconsciouskid.org/blog

The Conscious Kid is a multifaceted organization dedicated to reducing bias and promoting positive identity development in youth. Social worker and researcher Katie Ishizuka and educator Ramón Stephens, co-founders of The Conscious Kid, published a study in 2019, "The Cat Is Out of the Bag: Orientalism, Anti-Blackness, and White Supremacy in Dr. Seuss's Children's Books," as part of St. Catherine University's Research on Diversity in Youth Literature.

Ishizuka and Stephens are on Twitter @consciouskidlib

DISRUPT TEXTS

disrupttexts.org

Disrupt Texts is "a crowd-sourced, grass roots effort by teachers for teachers to challenge the traditional canon in order to create a more inclusive, representative, and equitable language arts curriculum that our students deserve." Tricia Ebarvia, Lorena German, Dr. Kimberly Parker, and Julia E. Torres, founders of the movement, connect with and support teachers committed to anti-racist/anti-bias teaching, and host a regular slow chat on Twitter with the hashtag #DisruptTexts.

Tricia Ebarvia is on Twitter @triciaebarvia
Lorena German is on Twitter @nenagerman
Dr. Kim Parker is on Twitter @TchKimPossible

Julia E. Torres is on Twitter @juliaerin80

DIVERSITY JEDI

Cynthia Leitich Smith, a member of the Muscogee Nation, coined the hashtag #DiversityJedi in 2015 after a white author called Dr. Debbie Reese, a scholar and librarian who is a member of the Nambé Pueblo nation, a "stormtrooper" in response to her criticism of children's books that misrepresent First/Native Nations' peoples, traditions, and histories. Reese, Smith, and others bestow the title "Diversity Jedi" on those who call out such misrepresentation. They also bestow it on those who call out "tone policing," which Edith Campbell says "happens during conversations or debates when one person, typically of greater privilege, thwarts a speaker's thoughts or opinions by reacting to their emotional tone," as Reese's opponent did.

Search for #DiversityJedi

LATINXS IN KIDLIT

latinosinkidlit.com

The mission of this vibrant website founded by author and educator Cindy L. Rodriguez, which features contributions from Latinx educators, librarians, authors/illustrators, and researchers, is "to engage with works about, for, and/or by Latinxs; offer a broad forum on Latinx children's, MG, and YA books; promote literacy and the love of books within the Latinx community; examine the historical and contemporary state of Latinx characters; encourage interest in Latinx literature among non-Latinx readers; share perspectives and resources that can be of use to writers, authors, illustrators, librarians, parents, teachers, scholars, and other stakeholders in literacy and publishing."

Latinxs in KidLit is on Twitter @LatinosInKidLit

Cindy L. Rodriguez is on Twitter @RodriguezCindyL

LEE & LOW BOOKS

leeandlow.com

Lee & Low is the largest multicultural publishing house in the United States and one of the few that is minority owned. It was founded in 1991 with the simple mission to "publish contemporary, diverse stories that all children could enjoy." Lee & Low makes concerted efforts to publish and promote previously unpublished authors and illustrators of color. Among the many valuable resources available on its website is an interactive Classroom Library Questionnaire that enables teachers to build diverse, culturally responsive collections by identifying strengths and addressing gaps.

OWN VOICES

corinneduyvis.net/ownvoices

In a 2015 Twitter post, Young Adult author Corinne Duyvis suggested that people use the hashtag #OwnVoices to recommend and discuss books by authors who share the identities of the characters they create. In a FAQ section of her website, Duyvis explains, "It's common for marginalized characters to be written by authors who aren't part of that marginalized group and who are clueless despite having good intentions. As a result, many portrayals are lacking at best and damaging at worst." Duyvis is also the co-founder of the Disability in Kidlit blog at http://disabilityinkidlit.com.

Search for #OwnVoices

Corinne Duyvis is on Twitter @CorinneDuyvis

WE NEED DIVERSE BOOKS

diversebooks.org

We Need Diverse Books is "a 501(c)(3) non-profit and a grassroots organization of children's book lovers that advocates essential changes in the publishing industry to produce and promote literature that reflects and honors the lives of all young people." The WNDB Executive Committee includes co-founder and CEO Ellen Oh, a YA author, and COO Dhonielle Clayton, author and former teacher and librarian.

Search for #WeNeedDiverseBooks and #WNDB

We Need Diverse Books is on Twitter @diversebooks

Ellen Oh is on Twitter @ElloEllenOh

Dhonielle Clayton is on Twitter @brownbookworm

4 Provide Ample Time to Read Every Day, Across the Day

A seminal study by Anderson, Wilson, and Fielding (1988) found the amount of time kids read outside of school correlated positively with standardized reading test scores. Yet, when reading outside of school, particularly at home, children are often distracted by smartphones and other digital devices, scheduling conflicts, and the daily din of family life. Moreover, as noted earlier, many of our children in poverty lack access to texts at home. Those time and access barriers combine to create an "opportunity gap" that can manifest itself in inadequate reading development.

To close that gap, school needs to be the place where voluminous reading occurs. We simply must provide time to read every day in school to ensure equitable opportunities for all kids, regardless of their income levels. To that point, Allington and Johnston (2002) suggest that students should be reading extensively across the school day. In this section, we suggest ways to make that happen, including not only independent reading, but also content-area reading, because reading is a knowledge-building act that is particularly important for striving readers.

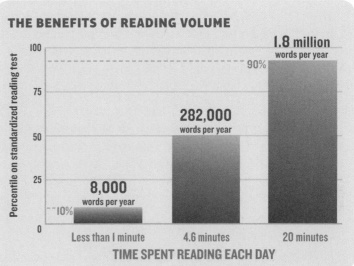

THE BENEFITS OF READING VOLUME

Percentile on standardized reading test

- Less than 1 minute: 8,000 words per year (10%)
- 4.6 minutes: 282,000 words per year
- 20 minutes: 1.8 million words per year (90%)

TIME SPENT READING EACH DAY

- **Begin the day with reading.**
  Smokey Daniels and Sara Ahmed (2014) have taught us the power of "soft starts," gentle transitions from home to school in which students settle in comfortably with one another and their teacher. Beginning the day with 10 to 15 minutes of independent reading enables kids to orient themselves and think about things that matter to them, while building volume.

- **Make sure your literacy block includes ample independent reading time.** We recommend prioritizing and safeguarding a minimum of 30 minutes each day following the mini-lesson for children to read books of their choice, while you kidwatch, confer, and monitor book-matches.

- **Reduce or eliminate nonessential accountability measures.** Ensure that virtually all the time for reading in your daily schedule is for students' unfettered reading, rather than "volume thieves," such as comprehension packets, phonics and vocabulary worksheets, and other inauthentic written responses.

Third-grade teacher Lena Wicker opens most days with a soft start, a soothing period of independent reading after students have arrived. Lena confers informally with them about their lives and book choices.

READING ACROSS THE CURRICULUM: WHY MAKING TIME FOR CONTENT-AREA READING IS CRITICAL

In reviews of the research, Cervetti and colleagues (Cervetti & Hiebert, 2015; Cervetti, Jaynes, & Hiebert, 2009) argue that "knowledge building is the next frontier in reading education" because "evidence is beginning to demonstrate that reading instruction is more potent when it builds and then capitalizes upon the development of content knowledge." As students build knowledge by reading, they create a foundation that supports ongoing learning and understanding. When they comprehend what they read, they augment and enhance their knowledge base. In turn, they strengthen their comprehension and confidence with existing and new knowledge. The more content knowledge they have, the more likely they are to grow it (Harvey & Goudvis, 2017). Ultimately, content-area reading is a highly effective way to build knowledge, confidence, and capability.

Here are some tips for successful content-area reading.

- **Build robust content collections that invite choice.** Readers are far more likely to be engaged if they have access to texts they can and want to read. For content-area reading, we subscribe to Dick Allington's (2009) notion of "managed choice." We manage students' choices by limiting the texts they choose to the content area under study, while offering a wide range of texts on that topic. Specifically, we assemble content collections that contain numerous engaging texts at a range of levels and in a variety of formats and genres, based on the curricular focus.

- **Teach annotation strategies while reading for learning, remembering, and understanding.** Sticky notes, margin annotations, and graphic organizers can all play a role in holding onto thinking while reading in the content areas. As they are reading content-specific texts, students take notes on both the information in the text and their thinking about that information. Typically, in a T-chart with the left-hand column titled "Information" and the right-hand column titled "Thinking," readers record what the text says and their perceptions and questions about it. We need to send strivers the message that their thinking matters!

- **Teach comprehension strategies and show readers how we use them in science and social studies, as well as in literacy block.** Comprehension strategies are the striving reader's superpower! Thinking while reading enables readers to build knowledge and understanding, and engage deeply in their reading. Strivers need strategies even more than proficient readers because they are more likely to encounter unfamiliar words and ideas. They can rely on those strategies to figure out difficult passages and hurdle the background knowledge gap. For more on comprehension instruction, see *Strategies That Work, Third Edition* (2017).

- **Encourage real-world reading. Make content-area reading relevant and fun.** Draw strivers in with new-car brochures when studying force and motion, maps for geography enthusiasts, pamphlets from historic sites when studying the American Revolution, etc. Check out *Inquiry Illuminated: Researcher's Workshop Across the Curriculum* (2019) by Steph and her coauthor, Anne Goudvis.

- **Build interest and intrigue with source sets.** Explore content with visuals, videos, infographics, podcasts, and artifacts, in addition to text. When we add listening, viewing, and handling to the mix, all kids have access to information.

5 Build a Reading Community

Many years ago, as a fifth-grade teacher, Steph attended her first NCTE conference and hit the jackpot when she attended a presentation by the late educational scholar Frank Smith, who introduced her to his idea of the Literacy Club. In his seminal essay, "Joining the Literacy Club" (1987), Smith describes an inclusive, welcoming classroom community where no one is excluded. He shares that young children are admitted into the club as junior members. None of them are expected to be skilled, yet, but in the Literacy Club, the social energy is palpable. Members gain an understanding of reading and writing in the company of others who are engaged in literate acts. They share their thinking with one another. They learn as their teachers read and write to and with them. They pay attention to our print-centric world. The authors they read become their writing mentors. A new club member is not viewed as less capable, but merely less experienced.

We notice that when teachers model their classrooms on Smith's Literacy Club, strivers begin to thrive. Here are some ways we build a vibrant reading community, where literacy is the main event—and all are welcome.

- **Create a print-rich, interactive environment.** As you flood the room with authentic, functional print, such as labels, signs, directions, schedules, and calendars, also consider creating learning walls where kids can share their poems, stories, research projects, and so on. If their work is not finished, let them stamp it "draft" or affix a sticky note to it that says "work in progress." Leave sticky notes and pencils near the learning wall so those who read the work can post questions or comments about it. When students are immersed in authentic, functional print—print that they create or you bring in—they feel at home as readers. The first step to becoming a successful reader is to believe in yourself as a reader, and environmental print provides many "I can read" opportunities.

- **Share your own reading life with your kids.** Kids need to know that we are readers who have our own challenges, as well as successes and pleasures. So talk to them about the text you are reading. Share questions you have about it. Let them know when you are moved by a book, as well as when you are not and have chosen to abandon it. Strivers in particular need to know that even for adults, sometimes reading goes well, and sometimes it doesn't.

- **Give booktalks routinely throughout the week.** When a new book comes in, share the cover, talk about the author, read the back-cover blurb and a few pages to fire kids up. When we honor books in that way, kids flock to them. Keep in mind the lessons about book snobbery described earlier and share a far-reaching array of books to reel in as many readers as possible.

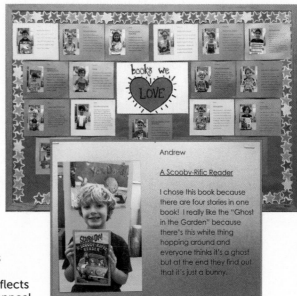

- **Recognize that good book recommendations for kids often come from kids**—and that sharing recommendations is a way for them (and you!) to learn about their reading preferences. In addition to your booktalks, invite kids to recommend favorite

Bernadette Tyler's first graders endorsed books they loved on a well-trafficked bulletin board. Andrew's selection of *A Scooby-Rific Reader* reflects Bernadette's openness to books with high kid appeal.

books on a regular basis. Remember to pay particular attention to strivers, who may lack the confidence to recommend books. You may need to provide them with additional encouragement and support.

- **Spotlight authors; engage in author and/or series studies.** Let kids suggest authors and series to study. Strivers frequently fall in love with a certain author or series and want to read them exclusively, which can be a powerful driver of their development. Series books in particular are effective at building confidence because readers are familiar with the characters, settings, and plot lines—making it easy to conjure up the background knowledge they need for the next book in the series. Author and/or series studies can be done with the whole class, small groups, or individual readers.

- **Incorporate authentic forms of response to books.** Our most natural and authentic response to what we're reading is to simply talk about what we have read. So, in addition to the student-led booktalks mentioned above, build in time throughout the day for students to share their thinking around reading. For a written record of that thinking, have kids write book reviews, which are published and read in the real world, rather than book reports, which aren't.

> **A NOTE ON POPULAR SERIES**
> The viral popularity of certain series at each grade level can pose challenges for striving readers, who may not yet be capable of reading them successfully. Seek out and consider reserving high-interest, mature-looking, but accessible series, such as those in the Scholastic Branches and Acorns imprints, for children in the upper grades.

6 Make Nightly and Weekend Reading the Main Event

Assigning homework—what we assign and how much—is controversial, but one thing is certain: The more we clutter children's backpacks with busywork, the less we support their independent reading at home. We need to make reading the main event, rather than something kids turn to only at bedtime when they are tired. In *No More Mindless Homework*, Kathy Collins and Janine Bempechat assert, "It's important that reading at home gives children a chance not only to practice reading, but also to grow a self-directed reading life, positive attitudes toward reading, and highly functional reading habits" (2017). We need to clear the deck and make room for reading at home.

- **Capitalize on momentum.** Kids are more likely to stay interested in a book and make headway through it when there is continuity between home and school. Through book-matching, you help striving readers find a compelling book. Make sure they tuck that book in their backpack every day and continue to read it at home. We mean this literally; make a point to check that kids have their books with them at the end of each school day, because this simple action is a powerful momentum builder, and strivers often miss out.

- **Reduce homework.** We send a mixed message when we call for 30 minutes of independent reading each night but send home a sheaf of worksheets to be completed, too. In our experience, teachers (including us) underestimate the amount of time it takes children to complete "paperwork homework." Meanwhile, parents prioritize it because of its tangibility. As one parent commented, "What's in the folder is what gets done." We therefore urge that you minimize other homework and help children and parents understand that nightly reading builds confidence and capability.

- **Engage families.** Communicate with families about books going home and the importance of reading at home. Make sure they understand that increased reading time will lead to growth. Urge families to designate a time and quiet place for students to read every day.

- **Reconsider traditional reading logs.** Given the importance of reading volume, we must know *that* kids are reading, *what* they are reading, and *how much* they are reading. Traditional reading logs, in which kids record each day the title, author, and pages they read, are one way to do that, but they may impede children's motivation to read. In our work with teachers, we've found several efficient and valuable alternatives to tracking reading, such as having students capture that information on their Next-Up Book List each time they read a book on that list. Another alternative is a laminated "What We're Reading" class chart (illustrated here) on which kids record with a dry-erase marker the author and title of the book they are currently reading so that you can monitor book matches, note how long children are taking to read their books, and form reading partnerships. It also enables kids to see at a glance what their peers are reading and learn of appealing new titles. (See Rethink Reading Logs, page 171, for additional considerations and alternatives.)

7 Encourage School and Public Library Patronage

The most robust classroom library does not have the vast and diverse collection of a school or community library, no matter how well funded it is. We believe that the school library is the beating heart of the school and the public library is the beating heart of the community. To offer students the widest possible selection of compelling books, we must tap the school and public libraries. Furthermore, librarians are invaluable allies. Partner with school and community librarians to determine kids' interests, book-match relentlessly, and maximize circulation. Make sure kids know that libraries and librarians are a never-ending resource they can tap regularly for recommendations, guidance, and publications of all kinds, in print and digital formats.

- **Teach students how to check out, reserve, and renew books.** Make sure each of your students has a public library card. Perhaps your school or district identifies a grade level at which to register children for cards. If it doesn't, register any of your students who don't already have cards. To ensure that library visits become a regular habit rather than a one-time experience, take students on a series of field trips to the library so they learn how to navigate the collection, use the electronic catalog, reserve and/or locate books, and check out and renew them.

These kids are using the electronic catalog to reserve and check out books.

- **Abolish circulation limits and eliminate fines in school libraries.** Many libraries are understaffed, and without personnel to process and reshelve books, they often limit the number of books a student can check out. Likewise, due to budgetary concerns, many school libraries don't allow students to check out new books if they have any overdue, unreturned books. In Mamaroneck, we studied the effects of that policy closely and found that it was disproportionately affecting our children in poverty. What could have been a vital lifeline for those children was not. For true equity and in the interest of all students, we need to do away with such policies.

- **Take advantage of digital options.** Teach students how to reserve, check out, and renew library books online. Also inform them about ebook options. With an ebook app, such as Libby, installed on their device, students can access electronic books anywhere, anytime.

- **Track library usage patterns.** While reviewing data from the Follett Web Circulation System, Annie and her colleagues noted a pattern that striving readers checked out books mainly during scheduled library periods, whereas thriving readers did so not only during those periods, but also before school, after school, and at lunch. Library patronage is an important agentive habit that can be taught and tracked. So, teach striving readers to avail themselves of the library whenever time allows—and track their visits and choices. Intervene with any children who are not yet active library patrons, as we'll describe in Chapter 3.

- **Create satellite collections, curated stacks, and special shelves.** Ask your school or community librarian to create a classroom "satellite collection"—an array of books on a particular topic, by a particular author, or in a particular genre or format. Invite the librarian to come in and present the collection, making a personal connection with your students in the process. Invite your school librarian to a wheel cart of tempting titles to your classroom regularly, book-talk them, and leave the satellite collections behind temporarily to augment classroom libraries, as Mamaroneck middle and high school librarians Kelsey Cohen and Tina Pantginis do. Confer with librarians about striving readers' interests. Ask them to curate stacks of books for those children to consider on library visits, as elementary librarian Lauren Geertgens does here. Nothing fancy is needed— just a special bin or a spot on a shelf and the gift of the librarian's attention.

Murray Avenue library teacher Lauren Geertgens has a shelf set aside where she places stacks of books she has curated for specific striving readers. Those kids drop by the library and hone in on Lauren's picks.

8 Promote a Leap, Not a Loss: Summer, Holiday, and Weekend Reading

In addition to ensuring that students have copious amounts of time to read when they are with us in school, it is vital that we set them up to read at home on weekends, school vacations, and over the long summer break. The phenomenon of "summer slide," whereby the reading progress of children from low-income homes stalls or regresses over the summer, is well documented. In fact, 80 percent of the achievement gap between middle-income and lower-income children accrues during the summer (Alexander, Entwisle, & Olson, 2007). We prefer to call it what it is—an opportunity gap— and eradicate it by ensuring that every child has access to appealing books when school is not in session for any extended period of time. What follows are some of the ways we do that:

- **Have students make vacation reading plans.** Long weekends and school holidays offer productive stretches of time for independent reading. Engage kids in planning ahead: get them talking about what they would like to read and where they will get copies (books or ebooks). Provide children with a blank calendar so they can make personalized reading plans that work for them. Confer with kids, particularly strivers, to learn about and support their interests and intentions. Teach kids how to find copies of their chosen books in school and public libraries, and consider procuring copies for kids whom you suspect lack access.

JAKE'S VACATION READING PLAN

When Steph visited Mamaroneck a few days before a school vacation, she guided fourth graders to make reading plans after modeling her own using the template she and Annie had developed. Not only did students leave the lesson with a workable reading plan, teachers gleaned valuable information to inform their teaching. Like Jake, many students had specific Next-Up books in mind and knew where and how they would find them. But also like Jake, some kids had an inkling of the kind of book they would like to read ("something like *In Harm's Way: JFK, WW2, and the Heroic Rescue of PT 109*") but sought book-matching assistance. Jake wrote "No idea" for the source, noting, "I like that it was about JFK, a survival story, and the photos/maps in the book," enabling his teacher to assemble a Preview Stack of on-target suggestions in time for vacation.

Using a blank calendar, Steph modeled how to plot specific and realistic reading opportunities around other commitments day by day, then invited kids to do likewise. Jake's plan revealed several interesting things that his teacher filed away for future book-matching: agency (demonstrated by his ability to select and download articles of interest from Newsela onto a family iPad), a book access stream (Grandma); and the ability to read in the car on long family drives. For more information on this topic, see "Making a Reading Plan" at scholastic.com/ReinventionResources.

Vacation Calendar with Reading Moments

Monday	Tuesday	Wednesday	Thursday	Friday	Saturday	Sunday
			19 Free Afternoon Start survival diaries avalanche	20	21	22 Family Picnic Newsela Articles
23 Drive to Canada Canada Year by Year	24	25	26 There is a lot to read in U.S.	27	28	29 Drive Home from Canada Newsela Articles

Vacation Reading Plan

Name: Jake

I plan to read...

Text	Source	Notes
Survivor Diaries Avalanche, Dust storm	library	I read Survivor Diaries Lost and Overboard. I want to read the others in the series.
Canada Year By Year	My grandma bought it for me	Im half canadian and Im going to visit my grandma in Ottowa, Canada
Something like In Harms Way: JFK, WWII, & and the Heroic rescue of PT109	No idea	I liked that it was about JFK, a survival story and the photos/Maps in the book
Articles About History and war	Newsela on my e-reader	Because I can read these on the go

- **Send students home with books.** The surest way to ensure access to books over school vacations is to send students home with a stack of reading material. Take time to book-match with your striving readers, drawing from your classroom library, and send each one home with their personalized collection, to be returned following the break.

- **Keep school libraries open over the summer.** Even if you send striving readers off with a personalized collection, it still makes sense to keep your school library open for them—and all students—during summer vacation so they can refresh or expand their collections. Perhaps a TV program has piqued their interest in a new topic, or a friend has recommended a good book. Also, for a variety of reasons, it may be simpler for your students to access the school library than the community library. To entice them to come in, host special events, such as an ice-cream social.

- **Organize book swaps.** If you have the time and wherewithal to curate donations, a book swap is a great way to circulate books without spending a dime. Put out a call for gently used copies of high-interest titles and set out collection bins. Plan to sort through what is submitted. In our experience, many donated books will need to be discarded for the reasons we describe on page 29. Once you've winnowed donations to books with currency and high kid-appeal, set up an attractive display in an accessible area with signage that invites families to take what interests them. Avoid "take a book, leave a book" language since there should be no condition for taking a book.

- **Promote book ownership through giveaway programs.** In a three-year study, Allington, McGill-Franzen, and colleagues demonstrated that book giveaway programs—with no accountability strings attached—are more effective than summer school in preventing summer slide for children from low-income homes (2010). Swayed by these powerful findings, the Mamaroneck Board of Education funds an annual summer slide prevention book fair, enabling all children eligible for free or reduced lunch to select and keep 12–15 high-interest books for summer reading. The Mamaroneck team has been tracking the impact of this initiative for years by conferring with participants and assessing their reading levels and are proud to have replicated the results of Allington and McGill-Franzen's study. In addition to mitigating potential slide, the initiative results in kids developing home libraries over time and taking pride in owning books that they love, that they chose for themselves, that they can access whenever they want, and rereading their favorites.

Students select high-interest books for summer reading from a year-end book fair.

9 Read, Know, and Share the Research on Reading Volume

Parents, and even some educators, often do not believe that kids get better at reading by reading. They never doubt that kids get better at soccer by playing it, or at dance by dancing, but somehow they have trouble equating voluminous reading with successful reading. It simply seems too good to be true. We must tirelessly promote independent reading and make sure parents and educators understand how crucial it is to reading development. Here are some ways to do that.

- **Share the positions of literacy organizations and publishers.** NCTE and ILA have produced research-based papers on the value of independent reading that are cogent, convincing, and readable. *The Scholastic Kids and Family Reading Report* contains essential information on reading volume, as well as other areas of interest to families.

- **Familiarize yourself with the research.** Encourage administrators or the school librarian to subscribe to print and/digital editions of periodicals such as *Reading Teacher*, *Language Arts*, and *Educational Leadership*. Pay particularly close attention to articles on volume and share what you learn with staff members and families. Divide and conquer; have teams across your school read different journals and share highlights at faculty meetings.

- **Read literacy blogs and follow educators on Twitter and other social media platforms.** Many routinely share research on reading volume and strategies to support striving readers. In addition to the suggestions on pages 35–36, we urge you to join Dr. Mary Howard and her wise band of literacy educators every Thursday night on Twitter at #G2Great to discuss literacy topics, especially those related to strivers.

- **On back-to-school night, present information about the power of reading volume.** Let parents know that their children will be reading a great deal in school every day and will be coming home with books to read each night, on weekends, and over vacation. Distribute handouts to parents on the research that supports voluminous, high-success reading.

- **Make sure your administrators understand the importance of independent reading for all kids, especially strivers.** Let them know that your students will be reading extensively and that much of your instruction will happen in one-on-one conferences with them, while they are reading. Share the research on volume so that they know the rationale for having kids read prolifically in school, every day.

- **Seek to duplicate the effects of research in your own practice.** Mamaroneck has successfully replicated Allington and McGill Franzen's summer slide prevention study. Track data of accelerated growth resulting from volume-based interventions such as book-matching and share with administrators.

By taking the actions described in this chapter, you create the conditions for voluminous, high-success reading. While it's likely that most of your students will thrive, some will require more support and qualify for supplemental interventions. In the next chapter, we describe how to use what you know about individual children to devise authentic and meaningful ways to amp up their access to books, choice, and time to read. By doubling down on those foundational elements, you foster students' confidence, reading identity, and agency.

CHAPTER 3

Interventions: Volume-Building Possibilities

Middle school librarian Kelsey Cohen scanned the circulation report she'd generated, yellow highlighter in hand. In the five years since the school had built classroom libraries and implemented a daily block of independent reading time, the school library's circulation had mushroomed, more than tripling in the first year alone. The numbers were impressive, and raised a question for Kelsey: To what extent were striving readers checking out books from the library? She highlighted each child who had borrowed fewer than three books across the year, and before long arrived at a troubling finding. She emailed Annie that afternoon.

> *Hi Annie,*
>
> *So I'm knee-deep in circulation data and checkout histories over here! You've inspired me to really take a close look at some of this, and I'm brimming with questions.*
>
> *I'm especially interested in kids who haven't checked out ANY books this year (GASP!) I have identified 61 sixth graders and 52 seventh graders—about 15 percent of the kids in each grade level—who haven't used the school library this year at all. Why?! We don't schedule library time for middle schoolers, the way we do for the elementary kids. If we lose them now, we may never get them back! I'd like to survey them to see what I can learn about their reading and book-choosing habits—and possibly identify any hurdles that may have implications for our library policies, collection, etc.*
>
> *I would love your input on developing the survey questions. I know the end of the year is crazy, but could we find a time?*
>
> *Thanks, Kelsey*

Kelsey's findings are yet another example of the Matthew effects that we describe in Chapter 1. While thriving readers were readily availing themselves of the school library collection, striving readers and children from low-income households were not. Kelsey knew she had to do something to disrupt this pattern and ensure that all students fished for books regularly in a well-stocked stream. After surveying students, conferring with them, and planning over the summer, Kelsey was ready to get *all* kids using the library when school reopened in September.

To promote library patronage from the get-go, Kelsey invented and launched the First Dibs Book Club. She pulled out a juicy collection of new books—unseen by middle schoolers—and invited a cluster of striving sixth-grade readers to a pizza lunch in the library. She displayed the hot new titles, book-talked them while the students ate, and provided browsing time. Kelsey used a Chromebook for quick and easy checkout. At the end of the lunch period, club members were stocked—and stoked—to read.

First Dibs Book Club

Based on the success of the First Dibs Book Club, Kelsey dreamed up other events over the year to lure in new patrons and load them up with reading material. Before winter break, she hosted "Ebookies & Cookies" to promote digital texts. Invitees received iPads repurposed from the district's 1:1 initiative. While students munched on cookies, Kelsey taught them how to download high-interest books from the public and school libraries for vacation reading, and made sure they had active public library cards in case they wanted to get more books while on break.

Kelsey's actions were powerful and proactive volume-building interventions. While many of the students she targeted were also receiving traditional skill- and strategy-based supports from teachers and interventionists, she created programs that pumped up their reading volume by increasing their access to and choice of books, time to read, and agency.

Ebookies and Cookies

Across the year, Kelsey tracked students who participated in one or more programs, using their elementary library circulation as a baseline because it came from scheduled library periods with built-in time for checkouts. Kelsey was gratified to discover that the majority of participants maintained or exceeded the circulation rate they'd had as fifth graders—meaning that they made time on their own to visit the library and borrow books. In essence, they became self-sustaining library patrons. One student, Ashley, increased her fifth-grade circulation by 50 percent in sixth grade, following her participation in the First Dibs Book Club.

Now that we've discussed the awesome power of the virtuous cycle (Chapter 1) and the conditions for all children to read voluminously (Chapter 2), we turn our attention in this chapter to interventions. Reading interventions typically focus on capability-building through skill and strategy instruction. While there is no doubt that children need explicit instruction to help them decode efficiently, comprehend deeply, and read fluently, it is not all they need. We're missing the boat if we don't pay simultaneous and equal attention to how much reading striving readers are actually doing.

Indeed, as Reading Hall of Famer Richard Allington asserts, "If educators hope to improve either the oral reading fluency or the reading comprehension of struggling readers, then expanding reading volume...must necessarily be considered. Considered as in evaluating the reading volume of every struggling reader as a first take to complete prior to attempting to design an intervention to address the student's reading difficulties" (2014). Not only should increasing reading volume be an intervention, it should be the first and most enduring intervention that we implement. Where and how do we start?

Reinventing Interventions

In this section, we discuss five actions you can take to reinvent interventions.

Embrace a New and Broad Definition of "Intervention"

in·ter·ven·tion | in-tər-ˈven(t)-shən *A caring, timely investment of intense, supportive, and outcome-changing effort.*

Look up "intervention" in our dictionary, and you'll find Stacy Peebles, literacy specialist, guiding Lila to find read-alikes. Lila had read and loved *George* by Alex Gino. Although Stacy had several books to recommend inspired by *George*, she showed Lila how to use Goodreads to find and explore books on her own and reserve those of interest from the library. This brief but powerful conference took place within a literacy support period. After teaching a whole-group mini-lesson on inferring, Stacy sought to build Lila's independence and agency by equipping her to search for books; as such, the conference was a volume-building intervention on its own.

Stacy releases responsibility to Lila, guiding her to search for read-alikes using her own laptop.

Here's how we expand the intervention landscape from the traditional RTI pyramid (at right) to a model that places the child and his independent reading life at the center. In her role as district Response to Intervention coordinator, Suzanne helps teachers understand the power of volume-building interventions alongside the more familiar capability-building ones. She created the circular graphic below to depict a more inclusive model that welcomes the efforts of teachers, librarians, aides, parents, administrators, and anyone else who increases the amount of high-success reading students engage in. It also recognizes that while an intervention may consist of an ongoing layer of support such as regular, small-group instruction from a reading specialist, it may also comprise a constellation of discrete, targeted efforts that remove barriers to volume, position kids to read, and create reading momentum.

TIER 3
MOST INTENSE SUPPORTS

TIER 2
INTENSE SUPPORTS

TIER I
FOUNDATIONAL SUPPORTS

Traditional Response to Intervention (RTI) Model

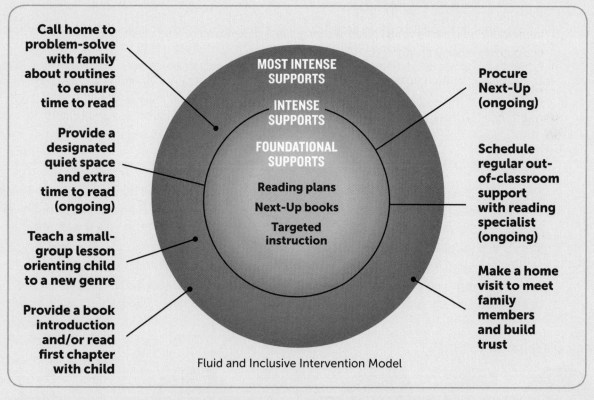

Call home to problem-solve with family about routines to ensure time to read

Provide a designated quiet space and extra time to read (ongoing)

Teach a small-group lesson orienting child to a new genre

Provide a book introduction and/or read first chapter with child

MOST INTENSE SUPPORTS

INTENSE SUPPORTS

FOUNDATIONAL SUPPORTS

Reading plans
Next-Up books
Targeted instruction

Procure Next-Up (ongoing)

Schedule regular out-of-classroom support with reading specialist (ongoing)

Make a home visit to meet family members and build trust

Fluid and Inclusive Intervention Model

Our RTI model moves away from linear tiers and takes a more fluid approach. A student's intervention plan can include both short-term and ongoing supports that range in intensity. The teacher uses her deep knowledge of the student in the round to design personalized interventions.

At the core of our model, a child's reading life is fueled by his teacher's volume-building efforts, which we describe in Chapter 2. The teacher prompts all children in the class to identify Next-Up books and make reading plans, and she provides whole-class and small-group comprehension strategy instruction. Beyond those efforts, the child benefits from additional interventions, including regular sessions with a reading specialist and a number of discrete and powerful volume-building efforts.

Book procurement: Knowing that this child lacks reliable access to books outside of school, the teacher regularly tracks down copies of his Next-Up books. Eventually, she will guide him to do that independently, but for now she keeps the books coming to ensure steady volume.

Book orientation: When the genre of a particular book is new to the child, the teacher provides a brief orientation to its features at the beginning of independent reading time.

Ushering in: To ensure that the child gets into the book, the teacher asks a paraprofessional to read the opening few pages aloud to him on the carpet.

Extra reading time: When the principal notices the child waiting for the after-care bus every afternoon, she invites him to read on the cozy bench outside her office, a volume-building daily interlude.

Family partnership: When she learned in a conference that the child is "too busy" at home to read most afternoons and evenings, the teacher calls his parents to request establishing a sacred time to read every day.

We don't typically categorize actions such as these as bona fide interventions. And yet these actions add up to high-success reading experiences that the child would likely not have had otherwise. Some interventions might happen only once, such as the ushering in. Others are likely to happen on an ongoing basis, such as book procurement and extra reading time. They all merit inclusion in the child's reading support plan, and their effectiveness should be tracked. More on that later in the chapter.

Adopt a Design Thinking Approach

The design thinking process is a human-centered approach to innovation that considers the needs of people first and foremost. In *From Striving to Thriving* (2017), Steph and Annie discuss the power of applying the design thinking process to work with striving readers, noting that it begins with empathy as the basis for innovative design.

When we empathize with striving readers, we avoid labeling them and presume they have boundless growth potential. We seek to understand their circumstances, without judgment. We define problems not as deficits in readers themselves, but as barriers to their voluminous, high-success reading. In this first phase, we pose and investigate questions to deepen our understanding of the challenges confronting each reader.

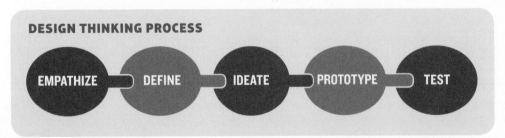

Adapted from Stanford D-Lab

A DESIGN THINKING APPROACH TO READING INTERVENTION

	ACCESS +	**CHOICE +**	**TIME =**	**VOLUME +**	**AGENCY**
Essential Question	Does the reader have abundant daily access to compelling reading material?	Does the reader have genuine choices to make in what she reads?	Does the reader have abundant amounts of time to read every day?	Is the reader accruing sufficient reading volume to set in motion the virtuous cycle?	Is the reader becoming more agentive and developing a reading identity from her time in texts?
Data Collection Through Kidwatching and Conferring	In conferences and reading logs, prompt the reader to identify the sources of what she's reading. Note patterns and gaps.	How does the reader describe the reason(s) for reading a particular book? Gauge her degree of investment in the book.	How much time does the reader actually spend reading? Does she use the time provided in class and seize other reading moments? How much does she read outside school?	How much reading does the reader accomplish in a day, week, month? Are you seeing evidence that she's entered the virtuous cycle?	Does the reader take initiative to locate books, discuss them, and participate in the community of readers?
Call to Action: Design and Track Interventions	If the reader lacks ample, reliable access streams, how will you open them up?	If the reader is not invested, how will you amp up her choices?	If the reader is not accruing valuable minutes of reading time, how will you set her up to read more?	If the reader is not progressing in an upward spiral of reading, what intervention(s) will you design based on one or more of those components?	If the reader lacks agency, how will you create the conditions for her to develop it as part of her reading identity?
Supporting Research	Entwisle, D. R., Alexander, K. L., & Olson, L. S. (2001). Keep the faucet flowing: Summer learning and home environment. *American Educator, 25*(3), 10–15. Neuman, S. B., & Moland, N. (2019). Book deserts: The consequences of income segregation on children's access to print. *Urban Education, 54*(1), 126–147.	McRae, A., & Guthrie, J. T. (2009). Promoting reasons for reading: Teacher practices that impact motivation. In E. H. Hiebert (ed.), *Reading more, reading better* (pp.55–76). Guilford Press.	Beers, K., & Probst, R. E. (2017) *Disrupting thinking: Why how we read matters.* Scholastic. (See page 136 on the benefits of an extra 10 minutes of reading per day.)	Allington, R. L. (2012) *What really matters for struggling readers: Designing research-based programs* (3rd ed.). Pearson.	Johnston, P. H. (2012) *Opening minds: Using language to change lives.* Stenhouse Publishers.

We brainstorm specific and constructive strategies in response to the data we've gathered, and we name and describe those strategies in a way that is understandable to others. Finally, we test the strategies by implementing them and watching, listening, and gathering evidence of their impact.

That approach enables us to use what we notice about individual children—the information we glean from kidwatching, conferring, and other sources—to develop, field test, and track promising approaches to volume-building by amping up children's access, choice, time to read, and agency.

When using a Design Thinking approach to reading intervention, it's important to anchor the strategies you implement to one or more volume-building elements in the chart on the previous page, citing research as needed to bolster and legitimize your approach.

THREE SNAPSHOTS OF DESIGN THINKING IN ACTION

1. The Appeal of New Books. Kelsey's idea for the First Dibs Book Club came in part from noticing that striving readers expressed particular delight in getting brand-new, compelling books, perhaps because it didn't happen as often for them as it did for their thriving classmates.

For example, when Annie visited Sabra Rivel's fourth-grade class and conferred with Manny (pictured to the left), who was new to the district, he told her that he had been reading *Tales of a Fourth Grade Nothing* at his old school, but "it had a different cover." He said he liked the new edition much more because of its cover and the fact that he was the first one to read it. Annie couldn't help noticing that he mentioned the book's newness three times during the brief conference. Hearing of Manny's enthusiasm, along with similar enthusiasm from other strivers, led Kelsey to design a new intervention. Why not see to it that strivers get "first dibs" on the latest, greatest titles?

2. The Absence of Judgment. When Maggie began book-matching with fifth-grader Mattias, she noted that he was averse to reading anything he thought his classmates would look down upon: a common problem that prevented many strivers from entering the virtuous cycle. After investing a lot of time and energy to find books in Matti's particular niche areas of interest, Maggie was determined to get Matti up and running in them, without fear of peer scrutiny.

To begin, Maggie ordered online, with Matti's input, several inexpensive fabric covers called Book Sox. She kept several in reserve, hoping they might catch on with other kids. At first, Matti shrouded his slim books carefully in the Book Sox. But soon Matti stopped using them. Annie noted

Matti's book bin and Book Sox

the Sox stowed in his book box, along with the Next-Up book Maggie had ordered for him about Ultimate Fighting Champions. Presumably, as Matti gained confidence as a reader, he was less self-conscious. Also, when Matti saw that his books appealed to other kids, he was less inclined to cover them. Interestingly, as Matti was discarding his Book Sox, other kids in the class started using them, leading to a brief but productive (and stigma-less) craze!

3. The Spillover Effects of Agency-Building. Early in the school year, Annie visited a sixth-grade English class, noticed that many students were reading school library books, and conferred with Eleni about her selection.

Eleni bubbled with enthusiasm about *This Book Is Not Good for You* by Pseudonymous Bosch. "This is the third book in the Secret Series. I've read the first two already." When Annie asked how she had come to use the school library, Eleni responded, "Ms. Tucker and Ms. Ramos take us for book tastings. Mrs. Malgiolio, the librarian, spreads out books, tells us about them, and lets us explore."

As Annie was jotting a note about the impact of book tastings, Eleni said, "Want to know something else? Over the summer I took my family to a farm using a pass I got from the public library. Mrs. Peebles showed us how. I planned the whole day. My baby sister got to pet a goat." Annie was struck by Eleni's pride and sought more information from Stacy Peebles.

"We take field trips to the public library across the year," Stacy explained. "Students get to know the librarians and library resources through on-site scavenger hunts and other activities. By the end of the year, they know their way around. In June, we make summer reading plans, and I show them that the public library has passes to local museums and attractions." Stacy concluded that Eleni must have taken her family to the Stamford Museum and Nature Center. Another student had visited the Intrepid Sea Air Museum with her family using a pass. Like Eleni, that child was proud, telling Stacy that tickets would have been more than 100 dollars without the pass.

Eleni developed agency through school and public library visits.

Agency—the ability to make things happen for oneself—is a powerful by-product of the upward spiral. Students who have it keep reading and actively reach for their next books. They recognize the library is a resource for them to draw on. When we teach a child to tap resources—to taste books and visit museums—we enable her to know that the world is her oyster!

Typically, the behaviors of thriving readers, the ones listed in the chart below, inspire productive, volume-building interventions. If thriving readers engage in those behaviors, what steps can we take to ensure that striving readers do, too?

THRIVING READERS...

- Anticipate reading opportunities and make plans to read.
- Always have reading material; maximize downtime.
- Procure Next-Up books.
- Seek recommendations.
- Read reviews and awards lists.
- Anticipate new releases.
- Select books for various purposes.
- Have sources of reading material.

- Have a sense of literary adventure; try new authors and genres. Connect with other readers through book clubs and partnerships.
- Respect others' preferences.
- Follow favorite authors, columnists, or bloggers.
- Contribute to the reading community via recommendations.
- Have reading rituals and preferred reading spots.
- Handle books responsibly.

Help striving readers develop these habits as well.

Intensify Volume-Building Interventions as Needed

In our opinion, a reading intervention is sound if it:

- boosts volume because of access to and choice of books, and time to read.
- heightens the reader's confidence, motivation, and agency to read.
- meets the individual needs of the reader.

When an intervention isn't yielding the desired results, the first thing to verify is that the reader is, in fact, experiencing its impact—that he or she is getting the "treatment." A striving reader may miss out on the benefits of a volume-building initiative if steps are not taken to ensure he or she is getting all the opportunities and privileges that the thriving reader gets. For example, striving readers and children in low-income households are disproportionately likely to have school and/or public library borrowing privileges revoked for not returning books or paying fines, thereby limiting access to books we presume they have (Peet, 2018). Here in Mamaroneck, when Annie and Maggie launched an annual summer slide prevention book fair for low-income children (see page 44), they were dismayed to find that many would-be participants were excluded at the last minute because they hadn't turned in signed permission slips for the bus ride to the fair.

Examples abound of well-intended efforts to promote volume. However, too many of those efforts benefit already-thriving readers, while failing to reach striving readers. Inviting kids to write peer reviews and display recommended books does indeed create book buzz, build community, and enhance the classroom library's appearance. But, chances are, without direct outreach to striving readers, those invitations are likely to be accepted by thrivers only and will be declined by those who most need to be drawn into the literacy club.

The first step in intensifying volume-building interventions is to verify that your strategies are reaching their targets. There is no doubt this is labor intensive. You might be thinking, "I'll never have time to do that for all my kids." The good news is, you don't have to! Many of your students, perhaps even the majority of them, will achieve reading volume if you carry out the foundational actions we describe in Chapter 2. But for the students who don't—and you know who they are— there is no substitute for going the extra mile.

In the next section, we provide seven examples of interventions that we have implemented, progressing from whole-class to small-group to individualized efforts. Note that the intensification "doubles down" on access, choice, time, or agency, rather than shifting to an entirely new approach.

EXAMPLE 1: BOOSTING ACCESS AND CHOICE

FOR ALL: Foundational supports	Open access to school library before, during, and after school.
FOR SOME: Intense supports	Invite students who are not yet patronizing the library to special book-matching events.
FOR INDIVIDUALS: Most intense supports	Curate individualized book bins and special shelves.

Mamaroneck librarians stock personalized book bins for striving readers, with the help of classroom teachers.

EXAMPLE 2: BOOSTING ACCESS, MOTIVATION, AND SUCCESS

FOR ALL: Foundational supports	Book-talk regularly and have kids keep Next-Up Lists.
FOR SOME: Intense supports	Make targeted recommendations to specific students.
FOR INDIVIDUALS: Most intense supports	Usher reader into his/her book; provide introduction; read the first chapter together.

Middle school literacy specialist Nancy Capparelli prepares to usher readers into hand-picked books.

EXAMPLE 3: BOOSTING TIME

FOR ALL: Foundational supports	Schedule sacred, uninterrupted reading time for all students during the day.
FOR SOME: Intense supports	Provide extra time for student(s) to read in school.
FOR INDIVIDUALS: Most intense supports	Work with a child and his/her family to develop a reading plan based on the family's commitments.

Keeping whole-class mini-lessons brief maximizes time for independent reading.

EXAMPLE 4: BOOSTING ACCESS, CHOICE, AND IDENTITY

FOR ALL: Foundational supports	Build the classroom library for the readers you expect.
FOR SOME: Intense supports	Customize and augment the collection to address specific students' capabilities, identities, interests, and preferences.
FOR INDIVIDUALS: Most intense supports	Hand-select, procure, and deliver niche books for specific students. See "Book-Match Plus: A Tailored Approach for Striving Readers" on page 57.

Kelsey Cohen orders books in all languages spoken by Mamaroneck middle schoolers. Here is a niche pick for "un lecteur aspirant" from France.

EXAMPLE 5: BOOSTING TIME AND AGENCY

FOR ALL: Foundational supports	Communicate to all parents the importance of independent reading.
FOR SOME: Intense supports	Call, email, or text parents and/or caregivers about specific books coming home.
FOR INDIVIDUALS: Most intense supports	Make a home visit to connect with the family and co-construct reading plans.

Naiomy read two books in two days! And she did a great job on today's lesson. She is bringing home 3 more books to read over the long weekend.

Thank you I am so proud of her. Thank you for everything have a nice weekend. 😊

Suzanne texts with Naiomy's mother to keep her updated about Naiomy's progress and to let her know that Naiomy was bringing home books to read over an extended holiday weekend.

EXAMPLE 6: BOOSTING CHOICE

FOR ALL: Foundational supports	Use varied source sets in curriculum units to provide choice for all.
FOR SOME: Intense supports	Provide choice of texts in guided reading and intervention lessons.
FOR INDIVIDUALS: Most intense supports	Locate or create enticing texts on niche topics of interest.

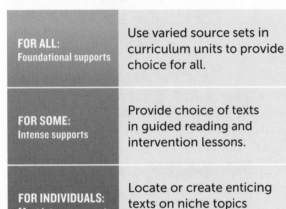

Kelly's teacher Liz Johnson assembles a customized text set on slime by downloading articles and recipes from reliable Internet sources.

EXAMPLE 7: BOOSTING ACCESS AND CHOICE

FOR ALL: Foundational supports	Guide all students to make summer reading plans.
FOR SOME: Intense supports	Procure and deliver books on specific students' summer reading plans.
FOR INDIVIDUALS: Most intense supports	Enable children without reliable access to books—including all children in low-income homes—to select and keep 10–15 books from a summer slide prevention book fair.

Friends stockpile books for summer reading.

Book-Match Plus: A Tailored Approach for Striving Readers

One of Maggie's summer responsibilities is to ensure that each new class section at a grade level is outfitted with a serviceable classroom library before school opens. One hot afternoon, she shared with Annie the challenge of stretching district dollars to create a baseline collection suitable for the range of readers in each class. Upon reviewing the children's June reading levels, she could plainly see that, while the majority of students were reading at or near the district's benchmark levels, there were some in every class who were not and would therefore need more accessible texts right away.

As she continued to pore over the data, Maggie noticed an interesting trend across the district. Of all the striving readers (i.e., those who were not yet "proficient"), 44 percent were assessed as reading only one level below benchmark. In other words, nearly half the strivers had relatively mild needs that could likely be addressed by stocking baseline collections with books at accessible levels.

The remaining 56 percent of striving readers in each class, however, had more significant needs; their assessed levels ranged from two to 14 levels below benchmark. Maggie recognized that virtually no amount of money would enable her to curate collections that would adequately match the capabilities and interests of those children. Furthermore, even if she did secure funding, the titles she chose would likely neither match the interests nor meet the needs of the following year's readers and would therefore go unread.

Maggie thought about the "book pantry" she had created for book-matching purposes—a centralized collection of high-interest books with low "effort-to-reward ratios"—and an idea took shape. She met with Annie to pitch it.

"You know about the online clothes-buying service, Stitch Fix, right?" Maggie asked. "Well, this would be modeled after it. Once a Stitch Fix professional creates a client's profile and learns about her wardrobe preferences, she curates a box of hand-selected items for the client's approval. The clothes arrive by mail, and the client keeps the items she likes and provides feedback about those she doesn't, which enables professionals to make more precise selections for future orders. Stitch Fix does it with clothing; we could do it with books."

Annie liked this creative idea, but was concerned that the arrival of a box to the classroom might draw attention to the striving reader's needs and be stigmatizing. She supported it, though, assuming teachers would find a discreet way for kids to receive their books.

Maggie identified a group of striving readers with whom to pilot Book-Match Plus, all reading well below benchmark, some emergent bilinguals and others on IEPs.

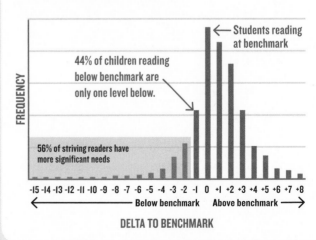

DISTRIBUTION OF STUDENTS' ASSESSED READING LEVELS

← Students reading at benchmark

44% of children reading below benchmark are only one level below.

56% of striving readers have more significant needs

FREQUENCY

-15 -14 -13 -12 -11 -10 -9 -8 -7 -6 -5 -4 -3 -2 -1 0 +1 +2 +3 +4 +5 +6 +7 +8

← Below benchmark   Above benchmark →

DELTA TO BENCHMARK

She designed an Interest Inventory for classroom teachers to use to identify each child's preferences. From the responses, Maggie identified six to 10 books meeting the criteria for each child. She retrieved those that were available at the school, ordered those that weren't, and boxed them up.

The district courier delivered the boxes, and classroom teachers shared them with the children in Preview Stack conferences.

(See page 111 for details on Preview Stack.) As each child sorted the books into yes, no, and maybe piles, the teacher asked questions to determine the specific elements the child liked or disliked about each title, recording her observations and the student's comments on a feedback form.

Each Book-Match Plus box thus served two purposes: 1. to get the child up and running with one or more high-interest books, and 2. to inform the teacher of his preferences, enabling her to make more targeted matches in the future.

Now in its third year, Book-Match Plus has been a smashing success! Rather than being self-conscious about the deliveries, children are thrilled by them and the attention they draw from peers. Fourth-grade teachers Debbie Schrank and Anne Marie Foley commented, "Jaden's face lights up when we sit with him to see what is inside his box. The

other students have taken an interest in his books, which has been a huge motivator for Jaden. The fact that his peers care about the books he's reading and think they are 'cool' and interesting makes him excited to read."

Not only have the Book-Match Plus boxes led to reading gains, as demonstrated in the charts to the right, they have led to notable increases in participants' agency and reading identity. Chantal's teachers Jean James and Bonnie Sloofman commented, "Chantal now reads to her younger sibling sometimes, which makes her feel proud. She talks to her peers about her books and will sometimes allow them to borrow those books, but only to read in class. She volunteers to read Morning Message now, and it's quite noticeable how much more focused she is when she's reading."

In its third year, Maggie expanded the program by recruiting and training a team of book-matching teachers, reading specialists, and librarians who are paid an hourly rate to "turn over the boxes" after school, meaning they receive the box, restock the books inside, review preference forms, and source a set of new books for the next delivery.

Interestingly, it takes 30 minutes on average to receive a box, restock its returned books, review the preference forms, and source a set of new books for the next delivery. Annie has pointed out to the superintendent that this is about the same amount of time as a typical reading intervention lesson. In other words, this volume-based intervention is no more time-consuming, nor expensive from a staffing standpoint, than other, more skills-based approaches.

During the shift to remote learning due to the COVID-19 pandemic, Maggie, Suzanne, and middle school librarian

ELEMENTARY BOOK-MATCH PLUS READING INTERVENTION PARTICIPANTS

2017-2018	2018-2019
34 children	**29 children**
• 31% students with disabilities	• 55% students with disabilities
• 36% English Language Learners	• 28% English Language Learners
• 67% children in poverty	• 62% children in poverty
September reading levels ranged from two to 11 levels below benchmark	September reading levels ranged from two to 11 levels below benchmark

IMPACT OF BOOK-MATCH PLUS

2017-2018	2018-2019
55% of children made accelerated or linear growth: • 36% accelerated (13/36) • 19% linear (7/36)	**76% of children made accelerated or linear growth:** • 52% accelerated (15/29) • 24% linear (7/29) **76% of students with disabilities made accelerated or linear growth:** • 63% accelerated (10/16) • 13% linear (2/16)

*See page 65 for a discussion of accelerated reading gains versus linear reading gains.

Kelsey Cohen revamped Book-Match Plus, coordinating librarians and reading teachers across the district to conduct virtual book-matching conferences and mailing or delivering more than 3,500 hand-selected books to students' homes.

Involve Students and Their Families in the Process

Another way we reinvent the intervention process is to place the reader and his or her family at the center. We open up and maintain an ongoing dialogue with the child's parents or caregivers about his or her reading life, and we collaborate to develop and implement a practical, volume-building plan that complements the rhythms of life at home. This involves identifying and maximizing daily and weekly opportunities to increase the child's access to and choice of books, and time to read. It also involves identifying and removing barriers to volume. The first steps are to get to know the child and his family, build trust, and establish a mutually convenient and reliable communication plan.

OPEN UP LINES OF COMMUNICATION

Once you have gotten to know each of your students "in the round" as we suggest in Chapter 2, it's important to reach out to your striving readers and their families more actively than you may with your other students. Here are some suggestions.

- **Confer with the child to establish a shared volume-building goal.** Assuming you've taught your whole class about the importance of reading volume, share your insights with the child and invite theirs. *Sam, I've been noticing that you've been having trouble sinking your teeth into a great book lately. Does it feel that way to you?* Emphasize your intention to support them in getting and keeping compelling material in their hands. *I'd like to work together to help you find book(s) that will grab your interest and make sure you have time and space to read them…*

- **Let the child know you will involve their parent(s) or caregiver(s) for support.** Emphasize that meeting goals, including reading goals, is easier with help from family members. In other words, the purpose of your outreach is not to punish the child or hold them accountable. *Sam, I'm going to let your mom and dad know that you're working on reading more at home so they can help you find the time. My husband helps me meet my goal of walking most mornings before school….*

- **Start with parents or guardians and involve others if and as appropriate.** Contact first whoever has legal responsibility for the child. Once you've opened the door, consider whether it would be fruitful to involve other adult(s) with whom the child has frequent contact. If the answer is yes, ask the parent or guardian who that might be. For example, in multigenerational households, it is common for grandparents to care for children after school. Depending on the family configuration and work schedules, there could be a babysitter, nanny, or high school-aged sibling whose support could be enlisted.

Be persistent and don't let language differences impede your outreach. In our experience, it is often necessary to try multiple means of communication before hitting on a winning one. Beyond email and phone calls, we have found that texting and WhatsApp are effective, unintimidating ways to reach many working parents. Services such as Remind and Google Voice allow you to send texts and make calls without sharing your phone number. If your school does not provide translation services, use an online translator, such as Google Translate, to reach out in the family members' home language and invite them to respond in that language.

CONVEY THE IMPORTANCE OF INCREASED READING VOLUME

Fortunately, the concept that one gets better at reading by reading a lot is logical and easy for both children and adults to grasp. Still, independent reading is all too often viewed as a pleasant "extra" once other assignments are finished. That's why it's important to be clear and emphatic about its importance.

- Assuming that you've taught the whole class about the power of reading volume as we suggest in Chapter 2, explain to the striving reader that increased access, choice, and time to read are key components of their support plan.

- Explain that to parents and caregivers as well: *I'm reaching out to enlist your support in helping Sam read more. Did you know that reading volume—the amount of reading that children actually do—is the most important factor in their reading success? I'm confident that Sam will take off as a reader if we work together with them to read more every day and across the week.*

WORK COLLABORATIVELY TO IDENTIFY READING OPPORTUNITIES AND BARRIERS

Engage in constructive, nonjudgmental conversations about factors that support and impede the child's reading life.

- What is the child's daily routine? Walk through a typical day, noting wake-up time, after-school activities, dinner, evening, and bedtime rituals; look for pockets of reading time.

- Explore the flow of a typical week including the weekend. Are certain days busier than others? Does the child spend time in different households due to divorce or childcare? Do they have lessons or familial obligations that take up blocks of time?

- What are the child's current reading routines, if any? How are they working? It's likely that consistent routines are not yet in place or are unrealistic. For example, many children report reading before bedtime after other homework is completed. Fatigue often sets in, curbing volume.

- Does the child have a safe, quiet, distraction-free environment in which to read? We find that this is a major impediment to volume for many striving readers, one that parents and caregivers may be instrumental in mitigating once they understand the importance of reading time.

CREATE A VOLUME-BUILDING PLAN FOR THE CHILD, WITH THE CHILD

A successful plan is realistic and specific, tied to the actual daily and weekly rhythms of the child's household, and it promotes access to, choice of, and time for books. For example, when Liz Johnson found out that third grader Aidan spent weekday afternoons at a local boxing gym where his father worked, she reached out to Dad to make sure he found a quiet spot there for Aidan to read. Notice in the sample plan on the next page that the teacher assumes responsibility with the child for their access to and choice of books, while the parent assumes responsibility for their reading time at home each day and across the week.

VOLUME-BUILDING PLAN FOR SAM

STUDENT'S RESPONSIBILITIES:

- Participate actively in book-matching conferences; make their likes and dislikes known.
- Be discerning; choose books that are of genuine interest.
- Notice and report when their preferences change.
- Keep a Next-Up list of books to read; update it regularly.
- Bring independent reading book(s) to and from school every day to maintain momentum and maximize reading opportunities.

- Read at home during "prime time" when they are alert.
- Prepare to read: get comfortable, limit distractions (e.g., use a "Shhh, I'm reading!" sign).
- Discuss reading with their family, peers, and teacher; make recommendations.
- Use the school library responsibly: borrow, return, and renew books regularly.

TEACHER'S RESPONSIBILITIES:

- Book-match regularly with Sam, using Preview Stacks.
- Seek out and introduce books in niche areas of interest (e.g., apex predators, reptiles).
- Procure books: get copies of high-interest books for Sam to maintain momentum.
- Prompt Sam to update their Next-Up list and make reading plans.

- Notify parents of specific books coming home: text screenshots of book jackets and provide a context and/or recommendations (e.g., "Sam read the first chapter in school with a cliffhanger ending; they are eager to find out what happens next").
- Meet weekly with Sam and communicate weekly with parents to report progress and adjust the plan accordingly.

PARENT/CAREGIVER'S RESPONSIBILITIES:

- Remind Sam to read for 30–45 minutes during prime time after school (e.g., on the couch while Mom or Dad prepares dinner).
- Keep siblings away while Sam is reading (i.e., Respect Sam's "Shhh, I'm reading" sign!).
- Limit screen time until after reading and homework are done.

- Read to and with children for 20–30 cozy minutes at bedtime. Turn off everyone's phones.
- Remind Sam to bring independent reading book(s) back to school every day.
- Communicate weekly with the teacher; send photos or anecdotes to track Sam's progress.

CELEBRATE SUCCESSES AND ADJUST THE PLAN AS NEEDED

Once caring adults start implementing the practical strategies, such as those described thus far, the child's reading volume will inevitably increase. The key is to keep the plan in effect long enough to launch the virtuous cycle described in Chapter 1. When a striving reader reads more across the day and week, he feels successful and proud. Additionally, his reading comprehension will likely improve which, in turn, motivates him to read more.

Regular check-ins between you, the child, and parent(s) or caregivers are vital so that you can note and celebrate what's working and tweak what isn't yet. We offer several caveats based on our experience.

- Urge parents to emphasize the intrinsic value of reading, rather than provide extrinsic rewards. Talk to the child about the book he is reading and encourage him to chat with others who've read it. Although it's tempting (and potentially effective in the short term) to provide incentives like stickers, prizes, or screen time, doing so is ultimately counterproductive (Kohn, 2018). Reading is its own reward!

- Relatedly, while tracking minutes and/or pages read may be part of the plan, remind parents that it's important to focus attention on pleasure and meaning rather than "how much." For example, consider the difference between a parent saying, *Sam, by reading an average of 40 pages a day you've read two books over the school vacation! You'll get to log them on the chart next week* and, *Sam, you've discovered an author whose books you really enjoy. Ms. Hoddinott says Arturo is also reading this series; you two will have fun comparing notes next week in school.* The latter comment focuses on the pleasure of reading, Sam's evolving agency (discovering an author and series he likes), and the social energy that comes from discussing books with fellow readers.

- Elicit and respect the child's insights into his own progress or lack thereof. Don't ignore anything that's working. In fact, call it out and name it in order to reinforce it. *Oh, you're finding that the non-soccer days (Tuesday and Friday) are reading 'mini-marathons' because you're able to read steadily for over an hour after school? Let's add that to the plan.*

The photos below depict ways families have celebrated and documented successful volume-building strategies.

(top) Araceli packs books for her daughter, Andrea, for all trips. She reports, "No matter where she goes, she finds time to read." (L) Andrea reading on the Metro North train after a family visit to New York City; (R) Andrea reading in the car on the way home from church

(bottom left) Elodia helped her daughter, Aimee, start a cozy routine of practicing reading with her brother, Antony, at bedtime. "She loves to read him stories before he falls asleep," Elodia notes.

(bottom right) Jennifer, mother of Daniel, Niko, and Jaylin, asserts, "Bathroom time is reading time!" She has found that when her children take refuge from their siblings in the bathroom, they will read if she keeps a basket stocked with appealing titles.

Track and Document Students' Progress

Intervention plans often focus on reading strategies, with no regard for whether and what the child is reading. Plans like that squander the meaningful, authentic, and motivating experience of reading. Therefore, we recommend that plans also include concerted volume-building efforts.

In this section, we show you how to incorporate volume goals and volume-building strategies in your plans. Set ambitious yet realistic goals for the number of pages, chapters, and/or books your students read, as well as for specific authors, genres, and text formats. Alongside evidence of reading, such as reading log entries, include information about factors fueling high-success reading experiences (e.g., watershed book series, productive reading partnerships).

Over time, it is important to assess the impact of your interventions. Combining formal assessment data with anecdotal evidence and your knowledge of the child will give you a complete picture of that child's progress.

STUDENT SUPPORT PLAN FOR: Hector
AREAS OF FOCUS: Reading Volume and Inferential Comprehension

DATE STARTED	GOAL(S)	INTERVENTION AND FREQUENCY	DURATION OF INTERVENTION	PROGRESS/OUTCOME
	(e.g., Strengthen decoding of multisyllabic words.)	(e.g., Guided reading 3x/cycle; small-group work 4x/cycle.)	(e.g., 6 weeks)	Include the date, assessment data, result (e.g., Jan. 1: running record/ student has met goal and/or new goal needed.)
10/19	Find time to read outside of school.	Created a reading plan and scheduled 30 minutes of reading each night	4 weeks	**11/16:** Over the past 4 weeks, Hector has followed his reading plan and finished 5 books.
10/19	Plan out Next-Up books to increase reading momentum. Find Next-Up books with more independence.	Use of a Next-Up Book List (every day after morning meeting)	4 weeks	**11/16:** Over the past 4 weeks, Hector has added 10 books to his Next-Up book list, and read 4 of these books.
10/19	Strengthen inferential comprehension by noticing how a character changes over the course of a story.	Small-group guided reading 3x per week 1:1 reading conferences 3x per week	4 weeks	**11/16:** Running Record Data: **10/26:** Level M, 98% accuracy and 5/9 comprehension (limited). **11/2:** Level M, 98% accuracy and 7/9 comprehension (approaching proficiency). **11/9:** Level M, 99% accuracy and 8/9 comprehension (proficiency).

In Mamaroneck, Suzanne has helped to guide teachers to document both volume-based and capability-based reading interventions in Student Support Plans.

- Assess the child's independent reading level formally and informally at regular intervals. For example, a running record with miscue analysis may be taken formally as part of a district-adopted assessment or informally by asking a child to read to you. In either case, the assessed reading level should confirm what you already know from working with and observing the child over time. See *The Next Step Forward in Running Records* (2021) by C. C. Bates, Maryann McBride, and Jan Richardson for expert guidance.

- Most assessment data are entered as static reading levels (e.g., measured in September, November, January, March, and June). While those are important benchmarks, be sure to determine if a striving reader is making accelerated progress to "catch up" eventually. Without calculating the striver's rate of progress, we could too easily be satisfied with modest growth when the reader is, in fact, "sliding" relative to grade-level expectations.

READING GROWTH: TRACKING RATE OF PROGRESS OVER TIME

1 Expected Growth

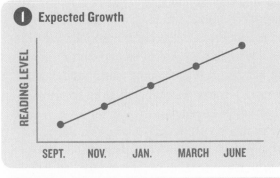

2 Linear Growth

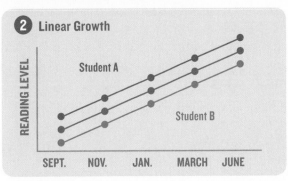

3 Accelerated Growth

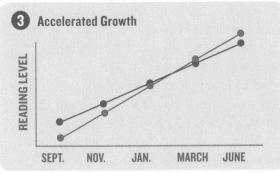

4 Negative Growth or "Slide"

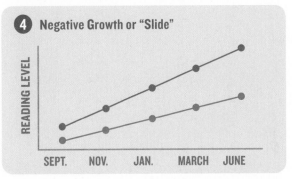

The graphs above illustrate reading growth. Graph 1 shows the expected growth for a reader at a given grade level, with a red line connecting the assessment targets.

Graph 2 shows linear growth for two readers, one thriving (A) and one striving (B). The two students' trajectories are plotted alongside district benchmarks in red, and all three lines have the same slope. The thriver starts out the year one level above benchmark and remains one level above, while the striver starts out one level below and remains there. Students A and B make linear growth because the slopes of their lines match grade-level expectations.

Graph 3 shows accelerated reading growth—or the "Holy Grail," as we call it! Here, once again, the district benchmarks are in red. The striving reader starts out the year below benchmark but makes dramatic gains. The slope of the blue line is greater than the slope of the red one. In fact, by March, the reader has met grade-level expectations. She continues on her accelerated trajectory and finishes the year in June, above benchmark.

Graph 4 shows the sobering phenomenon of slide. Here, the striving reader starts the year reading below benchmark. She makes gains across the year, but the gap between her capabilities and district expectations widens over time. Worse yet, the reader's slide may go undetected by her teacher and anyone else looking at reading data, unless it is plotted like this because she is making gains. Without looking at reading rate, educators can easily be heartened by modest gains, without realizing that those gains are inadequate.

In Mamaroneck, we created a tool to calculate the delta (distance in number of levels) to benchmark and rate of progress for individual students since last assessed for their independent reading level. The tool highlights in gradations of red students who are experiencing moderate to severe slide and highlights in green students who are making accelerated gains. In the partial class roster on the next page, notice that Bill and Jose entered below benchmark in September, reading at Levels G and H, respectively. Although both children maintained those levels from September to

Name	September Ind. Level	January Ind. Level	Delta September	Delta January	Rate of Growth
Barrett	G	H	-2	-2	0
Bill	G	G	-2	-3	-1
Marie	F	H	-3	-2	1
Olivia	K	L	2	2	0
Eric	H	L	-1	2	3
Keanu	G	I	-2	-1	1
Ariana	J	L	2	0	2
Camille	K	L	2	2	0
Ryan	I	J	0	0	0
Sophia	K	L	2	2	0
Alex	G	J	-2	0	2
Elvis	G	H	-2	-2	0
Anthony	D	G	-5	-3	2
Kaitlyn	F	H	-3	-2	1
Cole	J	K	1	1	0
James	J	J	1	0	-1
Scott	K	K	2	1	-1
Valentina	H	I	-1	-1	0
Jose	H	H	-1	-2	-1

- ☐ one level below benchmark
- ☐ two or more levels below benchmark
- ☐ moderate to severe slide
- ☐ accelerated gains

January, they "slid" relative to the benchmark; their rates of growth are flagged in red as -1. Also of concern are Barrett and Elvis, who entered school reading two levels below benchmark. Although they both advanced a level from September to January, their gains were linear; neither child has begun to "catch up." Their progress needs to be accelerated with voluminous reading.

Notably, six students—Marie, Eric, Keanu, Alex, Anthony, and Kaitlyn—made accelerated gains between September and January. All six entered school below benchmark. Alex caught up and reached benchmark in January. Eric not only caught up, he surpassed the benchmark expectation in January.

Our point is simple: When working with striving readers, we mustn't settle for anything less than accelerated gains. We must hold ourselves and our systems accountable for each child's growth. We are proud of our district's results, because it appears that as a system, we are getting better at accelerating students' progress. In a recent school year, more than half of children who were striving in September made accelerated gains across the year, with their teachers' support. Nearly a third of the strivers caught up, meeting or exceeding benchmark expectations by June.

ACCELERATED READING GROWTH FROM SEPTEMBER TO JUNE

	2016–2017	2017–2018	2018–2019
Students below benchmark in September who made accelerated gains from September to June	**44%** 218	**50%** 250	**52%** 279
Students in poverty below benchmark in September who made accelerated gains from September to June	**35%** 65	**43%** 88	**49%** 97

Of 532 children below benchmark in September 2018, 166, or 31 percent, ended at or above benchmark in June.

What is most important is that each child has grown as a reader because of his or her time reading books—has developed empathy, learned about the world, and become a confident and capable reader. The sections to come contain practical tools and strategies to support you in putting all children on vibrant and productive reading paths.

Part II

ASSESS: Diagnostic Questions and Instructional Options

In Part II, we invite you to study the readers in your class and identify those who would benefit from your urgent and supportive attention. Then, with a specific student in mind, we encourage you to use the Volume Decision Tree on page 72 to identify specific instructional options for volume-based interventions.

 Visit **scholastic.com/ReinventionResources** for downloadable forms, videos with the authors, and more!

Select Students Who Would Benefit From Intervention

Each fall, you likely begin the year by administering formal assessments that measure your students' reading capabilities. Those assessments are important, but they paint an incomplete portrait of your students' reading profiles. The tools that follow will allow you to complete the picture by measuring reading volume. This information will help you to identify children who would benefit from your immediate support in building a robust independent reading life using the tools in the remainder of this book.

OBSERVATION CHART

We recommend that you start with the Observation Chart to get a general sense of your students' independent reading lives. Over the course of a few days, as you notice various behaviors, make notes on the chart. Then examine your notes looking for students, especially striving readers, whom you suspect may need support accruing reading volume. See page 69.

VOLUME TRACKER

Next, use the Volume Tracker to gain a realistic picture of the amount of time those students actually spend reading. In our experience, the children who need the most time to read often receive the least, despite our best efforts to carve out time for independent reading across the day. See page 70.

VOLUME CONFERENCE

Make note of strivers who are not yet reading voluminously, and consider the value of conducting a Volume Conference to understand individual students' roadblocks to volume more deeply. See page 71.

At this point, you will have a deep understanding of your students' reading capabilities *and* the reading volume they are currently accruing. Consider which student would benefit from your immediate intervention, and dive into the Volume Decision Tree on page 72 with that child in mind.

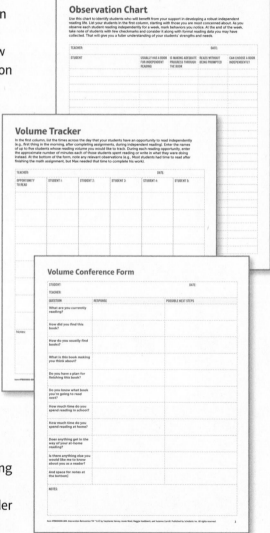

Go to scholastic.com/Reinvention Resources for these forms.

Observation Chart

Use this chart to identify students who will benefit from your support in developing a robust independent reading life. List your students in the first column, starting with those you are most concerned about. As you observe each student reading independently for a week, mark behaviors you notice. At the end of the week, take note of students with few check marks and consider this information along with formal reading data you may have collected. That will give you a fuller understanding of your students' strengths and needs.

Observation Chart

Use this chart to identify students who will benefit from your support in developing a robust independent reading life. List your students in the first column, starting with those you are most concerned about. As you observe each student reading independently for a week, mark behaviors you notice. At the end of the week, take note of students with few checkmarks and consider it along with formal reading data you may have collected. That will give you a fuller understanding of your students' strengths and needs.

TEACHER: Ms. Driver   DATE: 2/9/21

STUDENT	USUALLY HAS A BOOK FOR INDEPENDENT READING	IS MAKING ADEQUATE PROGRESS THROUGH THE BOOK	READS WITHOUT BEING PROMPTED	CAN CHOOSE A BOOK INDEPENDENTLY
Ivan	✓	✓		✓
Natalia	✓	✓	✓	✓
Tommy				
Laura	✓	✓	✓	✓
Sammy	✓	✓	✓	✓
Alejandro	✓	✓	✓	✓
Orée			✓	
Giuseppe	✓	✓		✓
Nigel				✓
Ayla	✓	✓	✓	✓
Daniella	✓		✓	✓
Isaac	✓	✓		✓
Jade	✓	✓		✓
Kenneth	✓	✓	✓	
Alex	✓	✓	✓	✓
Thea			✓	✓
Ella	✓	✓	✓	✓
Angie	✓	✓	✓	✓
Lily	✓	✓		✓
Joel				
Catherine	✓	✓	✓	✓
Jeremy	✓	✓	✓	✓
Nikolas	✓		✓	✓
Jody	✓	✓	✓	

scholastic.com/ReinventionResources

Volume Tracker

Quantifying the amount of time individual students have to read during the school day can be eye opening, particularly when we pay close attention to striving readers who often leave the classroom for interventions. Even in classrooms where independent reading is prioritized, we find that striving readers often do not have sufficient opportunities to read.

VOLUME-BUILDING FOCUS

- Time

GOAL

- To gain a realistic picture of the number of minutes students spend reading across the day.

YOU MIGHT TRY THIS IF...

- you are interested in learning how many minutes students are actually reading across the school day.

GROUP SIZE

- One to five students

PREPARATION

- Make a copy of the Volume Tracker at scholastic.com/ReinventionResources.
- Select a typical day when you anticipate students will engage in independent reading as they normally would.
- Select one to five students about whose independent reading lives you have questions.
- List these students' names in the Volume Tracker.
- List all of the times in the school day when students might read independently (e.g., after unpacking for the day, after finishing the initial do-now assignment, during each transition). Leave some spaces blank for times that you didn't anticipate. If any of the students you are observing leave class for pull-out instruction, try to collaborate with other teachers the children to work with to track their volume outside of the classroom.

STEPS

- Keep the form on a clipboard or device and commit to carry it with you everywhere you go for a single day.
- Every time students have an opportunity to read (e.g., first thing in the morning, after completing assignments, during independent reading), note the approximate number of minutes each child reads or make note of other behaviors (e.g., going to the bathroom, looking for a book).
- Fill in the time when that reading opportunity ends.
- Analyze the data and decide on next steps.

TIP

- Have students keep their own Volume Tracker to use across their day in and out of school as a self-assessment. This will help you to recognize students who need support in finding time to read.

NEXT STEP

Decide which student would benefit from your immediate attention. You can either:

Turn to page 71 to conduct a **Volume Conference** if you would like to gather more information about this student's independent reading life.

Turn to page 72 to begin making your way through the **Volume Decision Tree** with this child in mind.

Intervention Reinvention: A Volume-Based Approach to Reading Success

Volume Conference

During a one-on-one Volume Conference, you and the student will gain a deeper understanding of her reading interests, preferences, habits, and access streams. That information will help you identify specific areas for growth and determine the level of support she might need.

PREPARATION

- Choose a student who concerns you, based on your kidwatching and conferring.
- Print a copy of the Volume Conference form at scholastic.com/ReinventionResources.

STEPS

- Begin by saying something like, *One of the things I like best about being a teacher is getting to know students. I would love to talk to you about your reading life. This will help me get to know you better, and it will help us both understand what's working well in your reading life and how I can support you.*

- Choose questions from the Volume Conference form to structure the conversation.

- After the conference, highlight areas that stand out as particular points of need and be sure to attend to these areas as you make your way through the Decision Tree with this student.

TIP

- Don't ask every question on the form. Use your discretion, based on information you need, to round out your understanding of the child's independent reading life.

Volume Conference Form

| STUDENT: | Nigel | | DATE: | 2/12/21 |
| TEACHER: | Ms. Driver | | | |

QUESTION	RESPONSE	POSSIBLE NEXT STEPS
What are you currently reading?	• Children's Encyclopedia of Facts	
How did you find this book?	• Classroom library • Has had in his book box for 3 days	
How do you usually find books?	• Classroom library	• Teach other sources for finding books • What are his access streams?
What is this book making you think about?	• Learning interesting facts (shared a fact about Neptune)	• Was not aware that book is organized alphabetically. Teach about book structure.
Do you have a plan for finishing this book?	I'm not sure yet.	• Observe for minutes spent reading each day and level of engagement / investment.
Do you know what book you're going to read next?	No.	• Confer about ways to find books. • Start "nextup" book list
How much time do you spend reading in school?	I read during independent reading time.	• Discuss other times to read (ex. morning ; pickup)
How much time do you spend reading at home?	• I try to read for 20 minutes each night. • Reading "The One and Only Ivan" at home	• Bring in "The One and Only Ivan" to confer • May need to make reading plan
Does anything get in the way of your at-home reading?		
Is there anything else you would like me to know about you as a reader?		
And space for notes at the bottom]		

NOTES:
- Schedule 1:1 conference and determine if "The One and Only Ivan" is a good match.

VOLUME-BUILDING FOCUS
- Access
- Choice
- Time
- Agency

GOALS
- To gain an understanding of the child's independent reading life
- To help students reflect on their reading behaviors, habits, and interests

YOU MIGHT TRY THIS IF...
- you are looking to deepen your understanding of a child's independent reading life.

GROUP SIZE
- One-on-one

NEXT STEP

Turn to page 72 to begin making your way through the **Volume Decision Tree** with this child in mind. Keep your notes from this conference handy to help you answer each Diagnostic Question.

Volume Decision Tree

MATCH THE CHILD WITH A COMPELLING BOOK

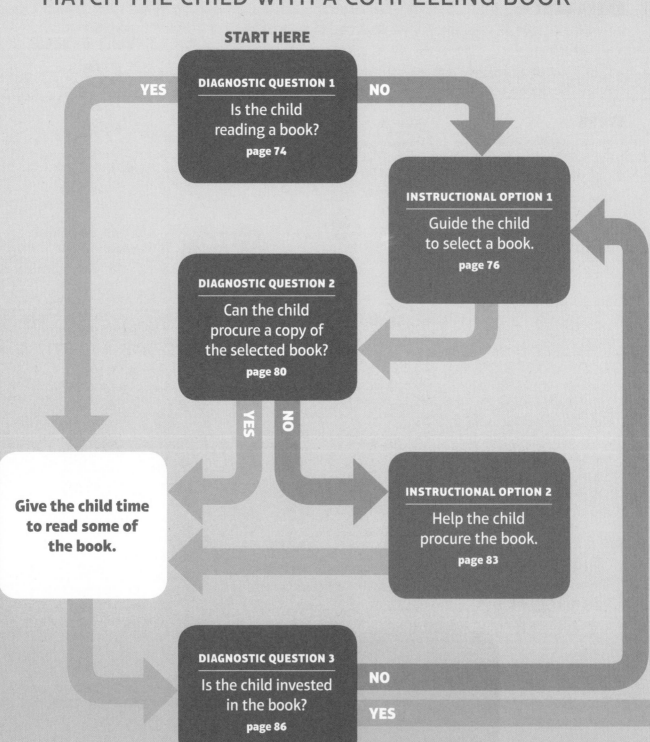

START HERE

DIAGNOSTIC QUESTION 1

Is the child reading a book?

page 74

YES   NO

INSTRUCTIONAL OPTION 1

Guide the child to select a book.

page 76

DIAGNOSTIC QUESTION 2

Can the child procure a copy of the selected book?

page 80

YES   NO

Give the child time to read some of the book.

INSTRUCTIONAL OPTION 2

Help the child procure the book.

page 83

DIAGNOSTIC QUESTION 3

Is the child invested in the book?

page 86

NO

YES

SUPPORT THE CHILD IN READING THE BOOK

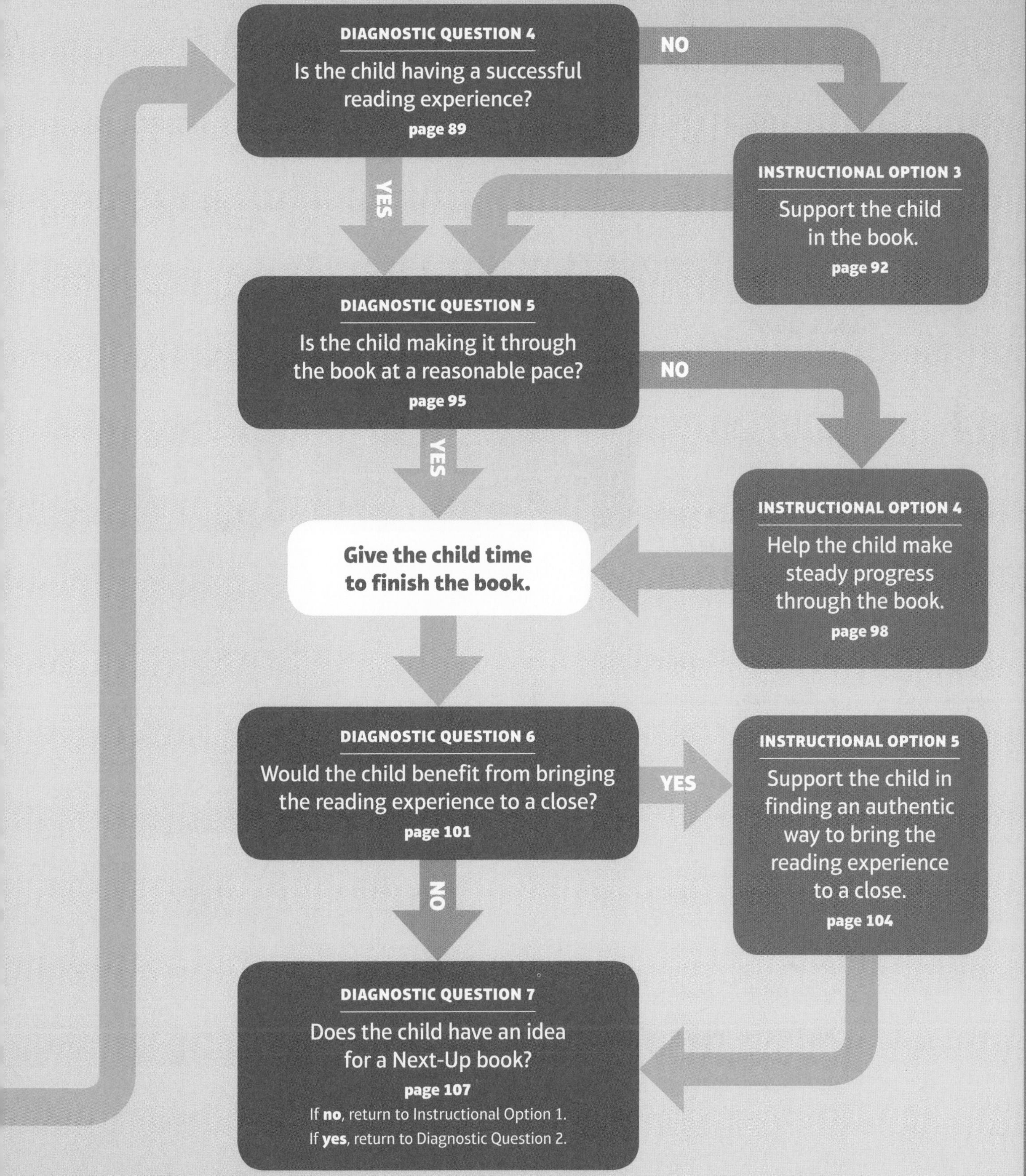

DIAGNOSTIC QUESTION 4

Is the child having a successful reading experience?

page 89

NO

INSTRUCTIONAL OPTION 3

Support the child in the book.

page 92

YES

DIAGNOSTIC QUESTION 5

Is the child making it through the book at a reasonable pace?

page 95

NO

YES

INSTRUCTIONAL OPTION 4

Help the child make steady progress through the book.

page 98

Give the child time to finish the book.

DIAGNOSTIC QUESTION 6

Would the child benefit from bringing the reading experience to a close?

page 101

YES

INSTRUCTIONAL OPTION 5

Support the child in finding an authentic way to bring the reading experience to a close.

page 104

NO

DIAGNOSTIC QUESTION 7

Does the child have an idea for a Next-Up book?

page 107

If **no**, return to Instructional Option 1.
If **yes**, return to Diagnostic Question 2.

Is the Child Reading a Book?

Why Is This Important?

All too often, we don't stop to consider this most fundamental question: Is the child reading a book? Before we can support students in becoming voluminous, engaged readers, we need to verify not only that they have a book in hand, but also that they're reading it.

Kidwatch

The simplest way to know whether the child is reading a book is watching her during independent reading or asking her directly. Nobody likes to do things that feel challenging or unpleasant. Children, particularly those who have not yet experienced the joy of a good book, often find ways to avoid reading.

As you kidwatch, ask yourself...

- When independent reading time begins, does she take out a book and start reading?
- Does the child keep her book close, ready to pick it up when an opportunity to read arises?
- Does the child spend much of her reading time shopping for books?
- Does she get up frequently to get a drink of water or go to the bathroom?

A reader who doesn't keep her book close at hand, or often leaves her seat during reading time, likely doesn't have a compelling book to read.

Confer

Ask the child about what she is reading to determine if she has a book to read.

What are you reading right now? An engaged reader can usually tell you the title off the top of her head or show you the book she is currently reading. A child who has difficulty answering this question likely does not have a book or is not well matched.

Consider

While we talk about reading books throughout Parts II and III, we support any reading that the child is invested in and motivated to read. Magazine or newspaper articles, websites, essays, recipes, poems, scripts, and more can provide vital stretches of engaged, high-success reading.

Collect/Track/Document

- Conferring notes or book logs that highlight the child's book choices over time. Look for patterns that might indicate the child needs support finding and making her way through books. For ideas on student-friendly ways to keep a record of books read, see Rethink Reading Logs, page 171.

- Photos of the child's book at the ready or tucked away.

RELATED READINGS

- Allington, R., & Gabriel, R. (2012). Every child every day. *Educational Leadership, 69*(6), 10–15

- Gambrell, L. (2011). Seven rules of engagement: What's most important to know about motivation to read. *The Reading Teacher, 65*(3), 172–178.

- Jennings, K. A., Rule, A. C., & Zanden, S. M. (2014). Fifth graders' enjoyment, interest, and comprehension of graphic novels compared to heavily illustrated and traditional novels. *International Electronic Journal of Elementary Education. 6*(2), 257–274.

Johnny was so enthralled with his graphic novel that he turned to it in the final moments of math class.

DECISION TIME

Considering what you've learned, do you think the child is reading a book?

YES

If yes, give the child time to read some of the book, then return to the Volume Decision Tree on page 72 and answer **Diagnostic Question 3: Is the Child Invested in the Book?**

NO

If no, turn to page 76 for **Instructional Option 1: Guide the Child to Select a Book**.

DIAGNOSTIC QUESTION 1

Guide the Child to Select a Book

Why Is This Important?

Stephen Krashen's examination of over 50 studies found that the single greatest factor in reading achievement is reading volume (2001). In short, if we want our students to become better readers, we must help them to read voluminously. Matching a child with a book that she can and wants to read is the crucial first step in reaching that goal. Two proven strategies for doing that are 1. offering Preview Stacks, and 2. teaching students to seek book recommendations.

Offer Preview Stacks

Inspired by the concept of Preview Stacks introduced by Donalyn Miller (2009), we have found that sitting down with a child to discuss a set of books you have preselected is a highly effective book-matching move. Although it's not uncommon for a student to leave the conference with a book she's excited to read, it's important to keep in mind that the ultimate goal of the conference is to learn about the student's reading interests and preferences. An added benefit is the personal connection you make with the child during the conversation.

If your kidwatching and/or conferring reveal...	You might...
• you don't know much about the child or her reading preferences • the child is no longer interested in books she used to enjoy	• **administer an Interest Inventory.** See page 110 for details. • **offer a Preview Stack.**
• you have done several Preview Stacks and are still having trouble matching the student with a book • the child frequently abandons books • the child would benefit from exploring how her reading choices have evolved over time • the child has been reading the same topic, genre, format, author, or series for a long time	• **offer a Review Stack.** See page 113 for details. • **consider the benefits of lingering in comfortable or familiar books vs. exploring the benefits of branching out into new reading territory.** See page 154 for details.

If your kidwatching and/or conferring reveal...	You might...
• the child is experiencing a lull in her reading volume, and she needs some inspiration	• offer a Jump-Start Preview Stack. See page 115 for details.
• the child tends to stay within her reading comfort zone even though she seems ready to take on different or more challenging texts • you think the child is ready to explore new topics, genres, formats, authors, or series	• offer a Gentle-Nudge Preview Stack. See page 117 for details.

CLASSROOM SNAPSHOT Fifth-grade teacher Michelle O'Connell was working hard to match her student Bella with compelling books, but after giving each recommendation a try, Bella often set the book aside and asked for something new. A Review Stack conference, in which they looked at a selection of books Bella had enjoyed, led them both to understand that Bella liked books about friendship, with lots of white space on the page and short chapters. Armed with that information, Michelle teamed up with library teacher Lauren Geertgens, and together they got Bella on a voluminous reading path by recommending a variety of graphic novels featuring tween girls navigating friendships.

Fifth-grade teacher Michelle O'Connell (left) and library teacher Lauren Geertgens (right) share a photo of Bella with the stack of books she read, thanks to their book-matching efforts.

Teach Students to Seek Book Recommendations

Seeking out book recommendations is a skill that will fuel your students' reading lives now and in years to come.

If your kidwatching and/or conferring reveal...	You might...
• another child in the class with similar reading capabilities and interests may be able to help her find a Next-Up book • social energy is building around a particular book, series, or topic, but the child has not yet been affected by it	• **encourage partner recommendations.** See page 119 for details.
• the child is ready to find books on her own but still over-relies on you for help • the child does not yet use resources to find Next-Up books independently	• **make Next-Up Book Lists.** See page 121 for details. • **teach kids to find Next-Up books.** See page 121 for details.
• the child is solely interested in one topic, genre, format, author, or series, and you are not sure whether you should encourage her to continue or nudge her into different texts	• **the benefits of lingering in comfortable or familiar books vs. branching out into new reading territory.** See pages 154 and 125 for details.
• your classroom library has books the child wants to read and can read, but she has trouble finding those books	• **take the child on an inquiry tour of the classroom library.** See page 127 for details.
• the child recently finished a book or series that she enjoyed and is having difficulty selecting a Next-Up book • the child has difficulty articulating her reading preferences	• **engage the child in book mapping.** See page 129 for details.
• the child frequently selects books that do not provide high-success reading experiences • Social energy is building around books that the child is not yet able to read successfully. You sense it would be productive to stir up interest in a new author, genre, topic, or format.	• **build book displays to broaden students' choices.** See page 135 for details. • **read aloud to build an inclusive reading community.** See page 137 for details. • **book-talk to build social energy.** See page 133 for details.

For students who require the highest level of support

If your kidwatching and/or conferring reveal...	You might...
• the child's reading capabilities fall well outside the range of books you have available	• **provide a curated book-matching experience.** See page 131 for details.

If you find yourself returning to this instructional option frequently, you should probably rethink the conditions for all students to read voluminously by...

- building a classroom library that provides access to a wide range of compelling, accessible books. This will free up time to focus your book-matching efforts on students who need more individualized support.

- auditing your classroom library for diverse and culturally responsive texts.

- choosing high-quality books for booktalks, displays, and read-alouds, including titles that even your most striving reader can read independently. Often, we showcase only sophisticated titles that leave striving readers feeling like what they can and want to read doesn't matter.

- understanding and honoring the elements of kid appeal—elements that make books irresistible to young readers.

See pages 27–36, 57–58, and 133–137 for details on those practices.

NEXT STEP
After using Instructional Option 1 to guide the child to select a book, return to the Volume Decision Tree on page 72 to answer
**Diagnostic Question 2:
Can the Child Procure a Copy
of the Selected Book?**

Can the Child Procure a Copy of the Selected Book?

Why Is This Important?

Once the child has identified a Next-Up book to read, the next step is to determine if he can procure it quickly while he is motivated to read it. This is especially important if the book is new, popular, or likely to be difficult to find. Book procurement is a high-leverage, volume-building strategy that should be part of many children's intervention plans. While our goal is always to foster independence, we are always watchful to be sure that striving readers have continuous access to books and the ability to procure ones they want to read.

Kidwatch

To determine if a child can procure a book, observe how he accesses books. Generally, we find that thriving readers have multiple access streams, whereas striving readers all too often find themselves in literal book droughts (Neuman & Moland, 2019) or what we call de facto book droughts, in which they are surrounded by books that are unappealing or too challenging. As such, most striving readers benefit from support in navigating classroom, school, and public libraries to help them build independence and agency in finding books they want to read.

After watching the movie *It*, eighth-grader Joey knew that the Hommocks library would have plenty of scary books to feed his new interest. Librarian Kelsey Cohen is seen here matching Joey with a copy of *Scary Stories to Tell in the Dark*.

As you kidwatch, ask yourself...

- Where and how does the child obtain his reading material? Does he bring in books from home, the school library, and/or the public library, or does he rely solely on the classroom library?

- In general, does the child show agency by taking an active approach to finding books, such as searching in the classroom library, reserving books, and asking for assistance when necessary? Or does the student take a more passive approach waiting for help to find a book?

- Does the child successfully procure books on his own?

Confer

Inquire about the child's access streams and his ability to procure books from the sources he mentions.

> **It looks like you got this book from the school library. Is that where you tend to get most of your books?**
> A child with reliable access streams can usually list a number of go-to strategies for procuring books.

> **How easy or hard is it for you to find books to read in our classroom library?**
> Even a well-curated classroom library can produce a book drought for, striving readers. Striving readers and children with unique interests may need your support to find books that meet their needs.

Annie noted the new, signed hardcover on Lilly Anna's desk because it was likely a sign the child had robust access to books outside of school. Lilly Anna excitedly reported she had been to a book signing at the local indie bookstore, where she had met the author. Lilly Anna's teacher confirmed that the family valued reading and had the resources to procure high-interest books.

> **It sounds like you want to read ___. Do you know where or how you will find a copy?** After posing this question, allow the child time to think through possible sources. After he responds, determine how well he knows his options and the likelihood of getting the book himself.

Consider

- Even when access streams are available to students, it is important not to make assumptions about the child's ability to procure books. A student may find it challenging to navigate the classroom and school libraries, get to the public library, or rely on family to help track down and procure books.

- Verify the child's level of agency in accessing books outside of the classroom. Note whether he would benefit from learning to borrow books from another classroom, visit the school library outside of scheduled visits, or reserve books from the public library.

- Ask about fines and lending limits that may be preventing the student from borrowing books from the school or public library. Children in poverty are disproportionately penalized by circulation limits, fines, and/ or borrowing privilege blockages due to missing books. This is an equity issue because families in poverty often don't have the means to pay the fines. School libraries should not block book access for families who cannot afford to pay the fines.

RELATED READINGS

- Harvey, S., & Ward, A. (2017). Ensure access to and choice of books. *From striving to thriving: How to grow confident, capable readers*, 87–120. Scholastic.

- Neuman, S. B., & Celano, D. C. (2012). *Giving our children a fighting chance: Poverty, literacy, and the development of information capital*. Teachers College Press.

- Catapano, S., Fleming, J., & Elias, M. (2009). Building an effective classroom library. *Journal of Language and Literacy Education, 5*(1), 59–73. https://eric.ed.gov/?id=EJ1068161

Collect/Track/Document

- Reading logs that contain a "source" column, prompting students to note where they have found books (e.g., home, the classroom library, the school library, public library)

- Observation notes that capture the child's developing agency around book procurement. Be on the lookout for behaviors such as asking a peer if he can read a book next or reserving a book in the school library.

- Library records that capture each student's borrowing patterns. Does he check books out each week? Does he check books out at times other than his designated library period? Confer with the school librarian to glean insights from his borrowing patterns.

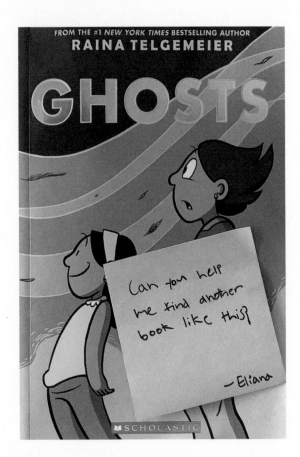

DECISION TIME

Considering what you've learned, do you think the child can get a copy of the book he wants to read?

YES

If yes, give the child time to read some of the book, then return to the Volume Decision Tree on page 72 and answer **Diagnostic Question 3: Is the Child Invested in the Book?**

NO

If no, turn to page 83 for **Instructional Option 2: Help the Child Procure the Book**.

Help the Child Procure the Book

Why Is This Important?

When a child is eager to read a specific book, he is on the precipice of voluminous reading. But too often, that momentum is stopped because he cannot get a copy of the book. Sometimes, the most effective way to support readers, particularly those who cannot tolerate lulls in their reading lives, is to procure books for them. As Nancie Atwell eloquently puts it, "The job of adults who care about reading is to move heaven and earth to put that book into a child's hands" (2016). Alongside these efforts, we also want to help students build agency and independence by teaching them where and how to procure their own. Two ways of helping a child to procure a book are 1. procuring the book yourself and putting it directly into the child's hands, and 2. developing his resourcefulness for finding books.

Procure Books for the Child

Sometimes your top priority is maintaining a child's reading momentum. When that's the case, it's important to locate the book for him and put it directly in his hands to propel him along the virtuous cycle described in Chapter 1.

If your kidwatching and/or conferring reveal...	You might...
• the child is excited to read a specific book but does not have a copy • the child has read everything of interest in the classroom library collection • the book the child wants to read is located somewhere he can't easily access on her own	• **see if the book is available in other classroom libraries or the school/public library. If so, reserve and retrieve the book immediately— get the book in the child's hands while he is still eager to read it! This jump-starts the child's reading life and signifies your deep care and concern for him.** As a student in Maureen Montone's class said when she handed him the book he sought, "You thought of me when I wasn't here!" • **load an eReading device with the text for or with the child.** See page 147 for more information on eReading.

Develop Resourcefulness

As the proverb goes, "Give a man a fish, and you feed him for a day; teach a man to fish, and you feed him for a lifetime." Similarly, if you teach a child strategies for finding books on his own, he'll be poised to read now and for the rest of his life.

If your kidwatching and/or conferring reveal...	You might...
• the child consistently obtains books from a single source, such as the classroom library • the child routinely relies on you to obtain books for him	• **let him know places he can find books for himself.** See pages 141–142 for details. • **teach him to become an active public-library patron.** See page 146 for details. • **make a practice of conducting home visits to build relationships with families.** See page 168 for details.
• the child's family is able and likely to procure the book for him (you have seen repeated evidence of a robust book access stream at home)	• **contact a family member with information about the book and ask them to borrow or purchase the book.**
• the child has read all of the books in his book bag or does not have books he wants to read in his book bag	• **consider flexible book-shopping structures.** See page 148 for details.

For students who require the highest level of support

If your kidwatching and/or conferring reveal...	You might...
• the child has not yet developed reliable access streams or agency for book procurement.	• **continue to procure books for him as you help him to build agency using the strategies above.** • **provide ongoing book-procurement support.** See pages 131–132 for details on Book-Match Plus.

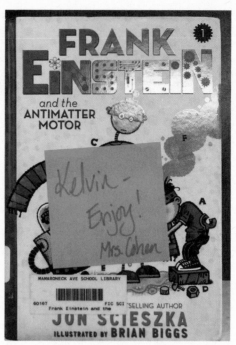

Annie was visiting Rebecca Streeter's seventh-grade English class when Kelsey Cohen popped in to hand-deliver a book for Kelvin, one of Rebecca's students. Knowing that the "iron was hot," Kelsey wanted to strike immediately so that Kelvin could start the book during independent reading time in English and take it home that night.

If you find yourself returning to this instructional option frequently, you should probably rethink the conditions for all students to read voluminously by…

- making sure the classroom library is weeded and easy to navigate.
- establishing flexible book shopping routines that ensure all students have access to a steady stream of books.
- teaching students to get the most out of the school library and public library, as well as the classroom library.
- helping students sign up for public library cards.
- teaching students to reserve books, search library catalogs independently, procure books through inter-library loans, reserve ebooks, etc.
- sharing books across classrooms.

See pages 29–31 for details on those practices.

Middle school literacy specialist Kim Armogida delivers a bin of manga books to a student learning remotely at home during the pandemic.

NEXT STEP

Give the child time to read some of the book, then return to the Volume Decision Tree on page 72 and answer **Diagnostic Question 3: Is the Child Invested in the Book?**

Is the Child Invested in the Book?

Why Is This Important?

Enthrallment is the ultimate volume-builder. When readers are invested in compelling books, they will engage deeply with the text, making meaning on page after page, an experience that will propel them along the upward spiral described in Chapter 1. Conversely, when readers are not invested in compelling books, they are likely to lose momentum.

That's why it's important to determine the strength of the "match" before proceeding with instruction. Our teaching will gain the strongest foothold when readers have a chance to apply strategies and skills in books with which they are deeply engaged. If a student's investment in their book is not palpable, we need to book-match until they find a more compelling title, rather than teaching our hearts out to get them through a book they do not want to read.

Kidwatch

One way to determine whether a child has a compelling book is to observe their physical connection to the book. Thriving readers typically keep book(s) close at hand, whereas striving readers do not. When a child has a book within reach, they are likely to be more motivated to read it. However, it is also possible that they have picked up the book casually, without any strong commitment or interest.

After reading every title in the Katie Woo series, Ashley was delighted when her reading teacher matched her with books from the spin-off series Pedro.

As you kidwatch, ask yourself...

- Does the child keep a book close at hand?
- Do they clutch the book with an air of interest, pride, and even possessiveness? Or do they seem indifferent or even vexed about it?
- When independent reading time begins, do they retrieve the book readily and start in?
- Do they appear to read the book with a sense of purpose, or in a casual, uncommitted way?
- Do they pick up the book voluntarily outside of designated reading periods?
- Do they make their way through the entire book before choosing another, or do they flit from book to book?
- Do they carry the book reliably back and forth between school and home?

Confer

Inquire about the child's reason for selecting the book, their degree of investment, and momentum.

I'm curious—what led you to choose this book? Listen carefully to the child's response. Investment is high when they have one or more specific reasons. Conversely, and concerningly, investment is low when the child shrugs or offers no reason or an unconvincing reason.

What is this book making you think? This question prompts the child to do more than retell; it prompts them to reflect and share their inner conversation. When a child is invested, they generally have lots to say!

Are you into this book? Is it grabbing you? This question reminds the child not to settle for a poor match.

Consider

When we labor to support kids in books that they are "just not that into," we face an uphill climb and misdirect our professional effort. In these instances, it may be best to guide the student into a new text. On the other hand, when motivation to read a particular book is strong, students are likely to put forth effort to make their way through the book. In these cases, it is important to support the child in the book. The next stop on the Decision Tree offers suggestions for supporting readers in books they are invested in but find challenging.

RELATED READINGS

- Gabriel, R., Allington, R., & Billen, M. (2012). Middle schoolers and magazines: What teachers can learn from students' leisure reading habits. *The Clearing House, 85*(5), 186–191.
- Guthrie, J. T., & Humenick, N. M. (2004). Motivating students to read: Evidence for classroom practices that increase reading motivation and achievement. In P. McCardle & V. Chhabra (Eds.), *The Voice of Evidence in Reading Research.* Brookes.
- Krashen, S. (2004). *The power of reading: Insights from the research* (2nd ed.). Libraries Unlimited.

TEACHER'S EFFORT TO SUPPORT CHILD IN BOOK

Vivienne picked a book from the library reshelving cart because she liked the cover, but she found it "boring." The teacher asks a few more questions, then conducts Preview Stack conference to make a new match.

Josh desperately wants to read a book from the I Survived series because it's viral in his classroom. The teacher provides book intro and reads first chapter aloud to set him up for success.

CHILD'S INVESTMENT IN BOOK

It behooves us to match the level of our instructional efforts to the degree of investment the child has in the book. Plotted above are two different decisions based on assessed level of investment.

Collect/Track/Document

- Conferring notes that highlight the child's level of investment with various texts. Look for patterns over time (e.g., higher levels of engagement with texts that have interesting call-outs, such as strange-but-true facts)
- Observation notes that capture the child's language about the book (e.g., "There was a part in Chapter 21 that almost made me cry.") and the child's reactions to the book (e.g., laughing out loud while reading)
- Photos of the child enthralled by a book during independent reading
- Photos of the child's books within arm's reach

These middle school students kept their books close, ready to pick them up to read as soon as they had a free moment.

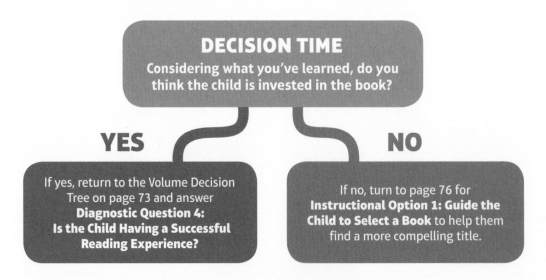

DECISION TIME

Considering what you've learned, do you think the child is invested in the book?

YES

If yes, return to the Volume Decision Tree on page 73 and answer **Diagnostic Question 4: Is the Child Having a Successful Reading Experience?**

NO

If no, turn to page 76 for **Instructional Option 1: Guide the Child to Select a Book** to help them find a more compelling title.

Is the Child Having a Successful Reading Experience?

Why Is This Important?

All children develop as readers through high-success reading. When a child faces significant challenges with decoding, fluency, and comprehension in a given text, she is unlikely to enjoy the reading experience or achieve the volume that she needs to thrive. That being said, sometimes children are highly motivated to read books that are challenging. It is important to figure out whether the child is having a successful reading experience to determine the best way to support her reading life.

Kidwatch

Children who are having a successful reading experience often show physical signs of engagement and investment. Those signs range from being hunkered down, quietly immersed in a book, to sharing an amazing passage or fascinating photograph with great excitement.

As you kidwatch, ask yourself...

- Does the student appear to be enjoying the reading experience?
- Does she react to the book (e.g., laughs at the funny parts, gasps at a plot twist, summons a friend to check out a cool illustration)?
- Does she read for a stretch of time without becoming distracted?
- Is she eager to share something from her book that may have touched her heart, made her think, or raised a question in her mind?

Fascinated and horrified to learn that some ants eat mold, Josh couldn't resist sharing with a friend.

Confer

Inquire about the child's level of success with the book.

Ooh, what's this part making you think? A child who is having a successful reading experience should be able to discuss a story's plot, characters, and/or setting, or explain information she has learned from a nonfiction text.

What do you hope is going to happen next? If the child is invested in the book, she will likely have strong opinions about the direction of the story, the information presented, or the position the author takes on a controversial topic.

Show me a part you really enjoyed or one that you can't stop thinking about. There is often a link between a child's level of enjoyment and level of comprehension. A child who is having a successful reading experience might connect emotionally with the characters, relish what she's learning, or be impatient to see what is going to happen next.

What are you learning from this book? Have you found any surprising information? When a reader of nonfiction has background knowledge on the topic, she is better able to engage with and comprehend the book. She also acquires new knowledge as she reads.

What has struck you? Sometimes when a child reads, she is simply struck by something— the stunning writing, an interesting idea, a character's actions, etc.

What are you wondering about so far? Are you curious about anything? A child who is engaged with a book will likely be curious about what she has read and will continue to generate questions as she makes her way through the book.

What, if anything, confuses you? Even a child who is having a successful reading experience may pause or stumble. Determine if she has any misunderstandings and work with her to clear them up.

Ask the child to read aloud to you: ***I'd love to hear you read a little from your book.*** A child who is having a successful reading experience will read with enthusiasm, fluency, and accuracy. Notice any problem-solving strategies she uses to regain fluency and accuracy.

Annie was tickled when Luke spontaneously offered to tell her a joke from the book he was reading: "Why did the flightless bird not laugh at the joke?" Answer: "He was not emu-sed." Annie asked how he had come to select the joke book from the classroom library, and he explained, "Every month I try to pick from a different bin. This month I'm exploring joke books and sports books." Not only was Luke reading successfully, he was reading adventurously.

Consider

- Reading with 100 percent accuracy and perfect fluency is not the goal; the goal is engaging deeply with the text and making meaning from it.

- Telling a child to stick with a book that she has lost interest in is counterproductive and can have devastating consequences on reading volume. When reading becomes a chore, reading volume suffers. Instead of judging a child's book abandonment, take an inquiry stance and guide her to select books that will capture and maintain her interest.

- If the child is reading a challenging text, be sure she:

  ▸ is invested and motivated enough to make her way through in a reasonable amount of time. If the child has lost interest in the text, the best option may be to guide her into a different text.

  ▸ has background knowledge that will support her comprehension.

  ▸ is constructing meaning as she goes.

Collect/Track/Document

- Video that shows the child reading aloud and/or talking about the book

- Anecdotal notes that capture highlights of your conversation

- Running record that captures the child's miscues and self-corrections based on meaning, structure, and visual information. See *The Next Step Forward in Running Records* by C .C. Bates, Maryann McBride, and Jan Richardson (2020).

RELATED READINGS

- Allington, R. (2009). *What really matters in response to intervention: Research-based designs.* Pearson.

- Krashen, S., & Ujiie, J. (2005). Junk food is bad for you, but junk reading is good for you. *International Journal of Foreign Language Teaching, 1*(3), 5–12.

- Rodgers, E., D'Agostino, J. V., Kelly, R. H., & Mikita, C. (2018). Oral reading accuracy: Findings and implications from recent research. *The Reading Teacher, 72*(2), 149–157. https://doi.org/10.1002/trtr.1686

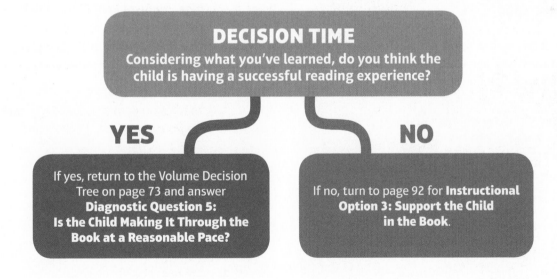

DECISION TIME
Considering what you've learned, do you think the child is having a successful reading experience?

YES

If yes, return to the Volume Decision Tree on page 73 and answer **Diagnostic Question 5: Is the Child Making It Through the Book at a Reasonable Pace?**

NO

If no, turn to page 92 for **Instructional Option 3: Support the Child in the Book**.

Support the Child in the Book

Why Is This Important?

Encouraging a reader as she navigates a challenging book benefits her in multiple ways. It promotes choice and agency and allows the reader to engage with popular titles being read by her peers. As a result, the child is more likely to become a member of "The Literacy Club," a term coined by Frank Smith (1987) to describe the social aspect of literacy. (See page 39 for more information.) When a child "joins the club," she connects with other readers and, even more important, identifies as a reader. Two effective ways of guiding a reader through a challenging book are 1. anticipating and discussing challenges and 2. collaborating with her family.

Anticipate and Discuss Challenges

A little effort often goes a long way to ensure students' success with challenging books. Demystifying new text structures, building background knowledge, and/or introducing the child to the characters and setting at the start of a new book can lead to an engaged reading experience.

If your kidwatching and/or conferring reveal...	You might...
<ul><li>the child is having trouble at the outset of the book, but you think she will be successful once she gets into it.</li><li>the child is venturing into new or uncharted reading territory, such as a new series, genre, or format.</li><li>the child is about to read a book with special features or a particular structure that is crucial to comprehending the text.</li></ul>	<ul><li>**ease the child into the text with a book introduction.** See page 149 for details.</li></ul>
<ul><li>the child is challenged by the book's unfamiliar content or format.</li></ul>	<ul><li>**build the child's background knowledge with photos, video clips, and/or companion texts that are easier to navigate (e.g., picture book or illustrated children's encyclopedia).** See page 152 for details.</li><li>**orient the child to the new format (e.g., each chapter is narrated by a different character).** See page 155 for details.</li></ul>

If your kidwatching and/or conferring reveal...	You might...
• the child is having a great deal of difficulty making her way through the book or following the storyline.	• **look for the book in a more accessible format such as a graphic novel.** See page 155 for details. • **see if an audio version of the text is available.** See page 151 for details. • **consider whether the child should continue reading the book or try something new.** See pages 125–126 for details.

CLASSROOM SNAPSHOT When third-grader Bea began reading the Owl Diaries series, Suzanne walked her through the first book and showed her how it is written as diary entries by the main character, Eva. She also pointed out the various bird-themed puns in the book, such as "I finished my Winglish homework."

Collaborate With the Student's Family

Fostering strong relationships with families is a powerful way to support children's reading lives. By helping families to understand ways they can support their child's reading at home as well as the types of books their child can read successfully, we can work together to ensure students have voluminous, engaging reading experiences.

If your kidwatching and/or conferring reveal...	You might...
• the child's family is encouraging her to read books that are too difficult.	• **recognize and share with families the benefits of lingering in comfortable books.** See page 154 for details. • **encourage family members to read aloud books that the child is invested in but not yet able to read independently. Encourage them to support their child's reading at home.** See page 157 for details.
• the child's family is judging her reading choices.	• **share information about the benefits of nonfiction texts.** See page 160 for details. • **share information about the benefits of graphic novels.** See page 158 for details.

For students who require the highest level of support

If your kidwatching and/or conferring reveal...	You might...
• the child is having difficulty starting a book, or needs support navigating a complex section of a book.	• read the book's first chapter or complex section to or with the child.

If you find yourself returning to this instructional option frequently, you should rethink the conditions for all children to read voluminously by...

- reflecting on your experiences book-matching with this child. Perhaps she needs more support choosing books that will be high-success reads. Perhaps she feels pressure from the adults in her life to read books that are above her independent level.

- taking a look at how often you are communicating with families about students' independent reading.

- ensuring that most books in your classroom library are at your students' instructional and independent reading levels, rather than at their frustration level. For more about that practice, see Chapter 2 and "The Leaky Faucet Case Study" in *From Striving to Thriving: How to Grow Confident, Capable Readers* (Harvey & Ward, 2007) and at scholastic.com/ReinventionResources.

NEXT STEP

Give the child time to read the book with supports in place, then return to the Volume Decision Tree on page 73 to answer **Diagnostic Question 5: Is the Child Making It Through the Book at a Reasonable Pace?**

Is the Child Making It Through the Book at a Reasonable Pace?

Why Is This Important?

As we stated in Chapter 1, Richard Allington (2012) defines volume as "the combination of time students spend reading plus the number of words they actually consume as they read." When a student lingers in a book for too long, he does not accumulate the volume he needs to move up the virtuous cycle. This is particularly problematic for striving readers who need to make accelerated gains. While we don't want readers to rush through books, we do want them to read enough each day to keep track of the story or content and to finish the book within a reasonable amount of time.

Kidwatch

Observing a child with his book over multiple days can provide valuable insights into whether he is reading it in a reasonable amount of time.

As you kidwatch, ask yourself the following questions:

- When reading independently, does he appear engaged for sustained periods of time? Does he turn pages at an expected rate?

- Does his bookmark move forward each day? If so, by how much?

- Does the child take his book home each day and bring it back the next morning? Is it apparent that he has read independently at home and made progress?

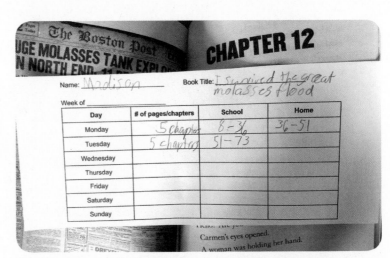

Fourth-grade teacher Jean James encourages students to set a goal each day for the number of pages or chapters they think they will be able to read at school and at home. At the end of each reading period, the children note how close they came to their goal on a recording form that doubles as a bookmark. Jean collects the bookmarks as a record of students' reading volume and uses the information to confer with students who need support making their way through their books.

Confer

In addition to discussing the contents of the book, inquire about the child's rate of progress.

It looks like you've been on Chapter 3 for a while. Why do you suppose that is?
As the child responds, try to discern whether the problem relates to the book (e.g., grappling with a confusing or dry part of the story, losing momentum or interest) or to other factors (e.g., having trouble finding a quiet/comfortable spot or time to read outside of school).

Did you find time to read your book over the long weekend? This question will help you to gather information about the child's home reading life and to assess any loss of momentum.

Are you still interested in this book? If the student indicates that a book is "boring," it may signal disengagement or confusion, which requires further inquiry.

I notice that you don't have your book in school today. What's going on? If a child often forgets to bring his book home or back to school, he may either need help with self-management, or he may have become disinterested in the book.

Is there anything at home that gets in the way of your reading? Don't assume that a student has optimal space, time, and quiet at home to read. Think about how you can support a student at home.

How far along are you in your book?
If a student is moving slowly, it may signal a lack of investment, or other reasons may be involved, such as limited time to read or noisy reading environments. Sometimes a child's reading rate may slow for positive reasons such as savoring the book or rereading sections. It behooves us to maintain an inquiry stance whenever we have questions about a child's reading life.

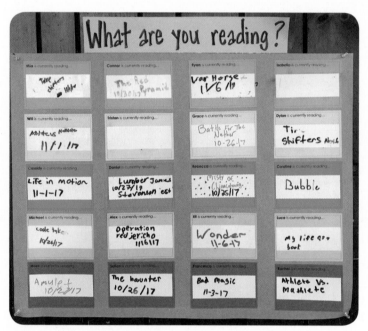

Fifth-grade teacher Ed Urso can see at a glance the books each of his students is currently reading. He uses the chart to inform his reading conferences, and he checks in with students when he notices that a title hasn't been updated in a while.

Consider

- If the child is not making adequate progress, consider whether this relates to the book or to the reading conditions.
- Investigate whether the child's reading environment at school and/or home may be affecting his ability to focus and read (e.g., noise, other students, siblings).
- Momentum and interest can wane even when an initial "match" was strong. Consider whether the book is proving too challenging or whether the child just isn't into it anymore.

Collect/Track/Document

- Reading logs or other artifacts that capture reading progress
- Observation notes that capture how long it takes the child to read his book
- Completed Volume Tracker. See page 70 for details.

RELATED READINGS

- Anderson, R. C., Wilson, P. T., & Fielding, L. G. (1988). Growth in reading and how children spend their time outside of school. *Reading Research Quarterly, 23*(3), 285–303. https://doi.org/10.1598/RRQ.23.3.2
- Harvey, S., & Ward, A. (2017). Pump up the reading volume. In *From striving to thriving: How to grow confident, capable readers* (pp. 121–139). Scholastic.
- Morgan, H. (2013). Multimodal Children's E-books help young learners in reading. *Early Childhood Education Journal, 41*(6), 477–483. https://doi.org/10.1007/s10643-013-0575-8

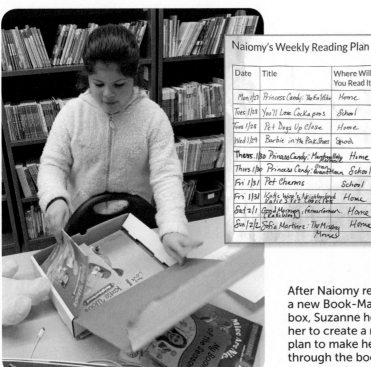

After Naiomy received a new Book-Match Plus box, Suzanne helped her to create a reading plan to make her way through the books she was eager to read.

DECISION TIME

Considering what you've learned, do you think the child is making it through the book at a reasonable pace?

YES

If yes, give the child time to finish the book, then return to the Volume Decision Tree on page 73 and answer **Diagnostic Question 6: Would the Child Benefit From Bringing the Reading Experience to a Close?**

NO

If no, turn to page 98 for **Instructional Option 4: Help the Child Make Steady Progress Through the Book**.

Help the Child Make Steady Progress Through the Book

Why Is This Important?

Continuously nurturing a child's reading volume is key to reading success. Volume provides children with the necessary practice to grow as confident, capable readers, but all readers hit bumps in the road, causing reading volume to decrease. When this happens, it is important to avoid making assumptions. Instead, inquire to understand the cause of the slowdown. This will help you determine the best path for getting the reader back on track. Two effective strategies are 1. ensuring copious amounts of reading time and 2. creating optimal conditions for reading.

Ensure Copious Time for Reading

Finding the right book for a child and getting it into his hands won't have much impact if he doesn't have quality time to read it. By carving our time for students to read and providing opportunities for daily independent reading, you greatly increase the chances of deep engagement with books.

If your kidwatching and/or conferring reveal...	You might...
• the child has limited time to read in school	• reflect on your daily schedule to determine if you're providing enough time for independent reading across the school day. See page 164 for details.
• the child is having trouble finding time to read outside of school	• work with the student's family to create conditions at home to fuel reading volume. Help the child and family identify potential pockets of time for reading. See page 157 for details.
• the child is moving slowly through his book	• explicitly teach kids about the importance of volume. See page 162 for details. • help the child to make a plan to finish the book in a reasonable amount of time. See page 165 for details.

Create Optimal Conditions for Reading

Environment matters. The right conditions set readers up for success. Physical comfort, noise mitigation, and solid habits and routines provide a foundation for positive reading experiences.

If your kidwatching and/or conferring reveal...	You might...
• the child starts and stops his reading • the child has difficulty sitting and reading for stretches of time	• take an inquiry stance when reading volume slows. Troubleshoot with the child to see whether there is something about the book itself or the child's physical comfort that is causing the slowdown. See page 161 for details.
• the child seems to be sensitive to noise and, therefore, has difficulty focusing on her reading when there is a "buzz" of activity in the classroom or at home	• offer the student noise-canceling headphones. See page 161 for details.

CLASSROOM SNAPSHOT Eric's fifth-grade teachers Donna Schore and Gina Ahearn reached out to Maggie to discuss some observations they had made about Eric's reading volume. Donna and Gina had worked hard to match Eric with the Timmy Failure series by Stephan Pastis and were pleased to see that he remained engaged with this series as he moved from book one to book two. Understanding the vital importance of reading volume, however, Donna and Gina became concerned when they noticed that Eric's bookmark was making very slow progress through book two. While discussing that issue with Maggie, they remembered that Eric lives in a small apartment with five brothers, an environment that made focusing on reading difficult. With a pair of noise-canceling headphones for at-home reading and dedicated time to read in a quiet spot in the classroom, Eric's reading volume picked up, and he made his way through the entire Timmy Failure series in just a few weeks.

Providing a variety of seating options is one way to help create optimal conditions for reading.

For students who require the highest level of support

If your kidwatching and/or conferring reveal...	You might...
• a student may not have optimal reading conditions at home.	• go on a home visit to build a strong relationship with the child's family and work together to develop a plan for the child's reading. See page 168 for details. • arrange for extra reading time for the student within the school day.

If you find yourself returning to this instructional option frequently, you should rethink the conditions for all students to read voluminously by...

- setting the expectation with students and families early in the school year that reading is a priority in your classroom.
- establishing collaborative relationships with students and families. Ask families how you can support students with reading in school and at home. Keep the conversation going across the school year.
- preserving and protecting time in your daily schedule for independent reading.
- providing choice so that kids are reading texts they can and want to read in the content areas.
- creating a system that allows you and your students to collaboratively track and reflect on reading volume, such as the status of the class.
- allowing the child to abandon the book and select another.

See pages 37–41, 167, and 171 for details on these practices.

NEXT STEP
Give the child time to finish the book ensuring that he continues to make steady progress, then return to the Volume Decision Tree on page 73 to answer
Diagnostic Question 6: Would the Child Benefit From Bringing the Reading Experience to a Close?

Would the Child Benefit From Bringing the Reading Experience to a Close?

Why Is This Important?

When we "hold students accountable" for their reading, we too often impose inauthentic and time-consuming tasks that rob them of reading volume and agency, such as answering comprehension questions and writing book reports. Instead, we should allow children to decide how they might best achieve closure after a reading experience. A child may want to move right on to the next book (particularly in a series), to discuss the book with classmates who have read it, or recommend it to others who haven't. Ultimately, we seek to offer a range of authentic opportunities that are as varied as our readers and books themselves!

Kidwatch

Rather than impose a response, observe what a child does naturally when they finish a book and support them in bringing the experience to a satisfying close.

As you kidwatch, ask yourself...

- Does the child return the book to the classroom library to find another one?
- Do they continue to keep the book physically close even though they have finished reading it?
- Do they continue to speak with you and/or their peers about the book?
- Do they seem reluctant to start a new book or seem to have difficulty finding one?

Annie Ward
@AnnieTWard

"Listen: If we're going to talk about dogs, we're going to have to talk about love..." Thank you, @JennyBoylan , for sharing your heart and soul—and seven unforgettable dogs—in these delightfully moving pages.

4:21 PM · May 24, 2020 · Twitter for iPhone

When Annie finished reading Jennifer Finney Boylan's memoir *Good Boy: My Life in Seven Dogs*, she was moved to Tweet a recommendation tagging the author. Annie was delighted when Boylan liked the Tweet moments later!

Confer

Inquire about the child's feelings about finishing the book and their readiness to move on:

Do you have a Next-Up book that you are eager to start reading? Too often, we unintentionally slow students' reading momentum by imposing accountability measures such as reading responses. If the child shows that they are on a reading path by having a Next-Up book they are eager to read, the best decision might be to let them dive right into that text.

I see that you've finished ___. What would you like to do now? Are you ready to move on to another book or not just yet? They may need permission to linger in the world of the book for a time. Listen for cues, such as:

▶ *I can't stop thinking about the people who were trapped in the Triangle Shirtwaist Factory fire.*

▶ *I want to memorize some of these jokes so I can tell them at camp.*

▶ *My friend Kevin already has the next book in Wings of Fire. He said I can read it next.*

Would you be interested in doing something more with this book? If the student expresses interest, consider the ideas in Instructional Option 5 on pages 104–106.

After reading *Dog Training for Kids*, Eliana was inspired to teach her dog Luna some tricks.

Consider

- Based on what they have told you, guide the student to either choose a way to close the reading experience or to select their next read.

- When a child is moving on from a particularly gripping reading experience, reminding them that they can always reread the book or revisit favorite passages will provide reassurance and help the reader to decide on their next steps.

- Reconsider any "must do" accountability measures that you have in place. While an efficient book-logging system may provide useful data to you and the children, anything beyond that runs the risk of deterring kids from reading voluminously.

Collect/Track/Document

Diverse examples of authentic reading responses:

- A recording of a student giving a booktalk to the class

- A photograph of an email or Tweet written to the author or a recording of the student Skyping with the author

- A student's Flipgrid videos reflecting on their recent reading experience

- Artifacts created by students to close out the reading experience (e.g., making a recipe after reading a cookbook; inserting a short review into the book for its next reader)

- A copy of a student's book review

RELATED READINGS

- Cunningham, P. M., & Allington, R. L. (2003). *Classrooms that work: They can all read and write* (3rd ed.). Allyn and Bacon.

- Marinak, B. A., Gambrell, L. (2016). *No more reading for junk.* Heinemann.

- Beers, K., & Probst, R. E. (2020). *Forged by reading: The power of a literate life.* Scholastic.

DECISION TIME

Considering what you've learned, do you think the child would benefit from bringing the reading experience to a close?

YES

If yes, turn to page 104 for **Instructional Option 5: Support the Child in Finding an Authentic Way to Bring the Reading Experience to a Close**.

NO

If no, return to the Volume Decision Tree on page 73 and answer **Diagnostic Question 7: Does the Child Have an Idea for a Next-Up Book?**

Support the Child in Finding an Authentic Way to Bring the Reading Experience to a Close

Why Is This Important?

When a child has finished reading a book that has captured their attention but is not yet ready to move on to a new book, we want to help them reach closure. We take our cues from the child and their reading experience and avoid traditional accountability measures, such as comprehension questions and written responses, which only serve to get in the way of reading volume. Two effective ways of supporting the child in bringing the reading experience to a close are 1. deepening the experience and 2. inviting others into the reading experience.

Deepen the Experience

When a book has captured the heart and mind of a student, finding ways to authentically extend their reading experience can deepen their comprehension and spark further reading.

If your kidwatching and/or conferring reveal...	You might...
• the child is eager to read the book again	• **allow the child to reread the book. Plan to confer with the child about new insights gleaned from rereading.** See page 172 for details.
• the child wants to know more about the content of the book	• **help the child find related informational texts, videos, or artifacts to learn more.** See page 152 for details.
• the child has questions about the creation of the book or wants to express their appreciation for it	• **contact the author and/or illustrator by email or Tweet. Many authors post contact information on their websites and love hearing from young readers.**

Invite Others Into the Reading Experience

One of the greatest joys of being a reader is sharing great books with others. Providing opportunities for students to bring others into their reading experiences helps them build readerly habits that will serve them for years to come.

If your kidwatching and/or conferring reveal...	You might...
• the book is not well known by peers, and the child wants to share it with classmates	• **offer the student the opportunity to do a booktalk for the class.** See page 133 for details. • **encourage partner recommendations.** See page 119 for details.
• the child is not eager to record finished books in their reading log	• **rethink reading logs.** See page 171 for details.

CLASSROOM SNAPSHOT Natalie and Carolina, fifth-grade striving readers, were both excited to have recently finished the first book in the Dory Fantasmagory series but did not have classmates who shared their enthusiasm. Maggie and Suzanne worked with the girls' teachers to arrange a weekly time for the girls to meet and talk about the book together. This informal reading club provided an opportunity to bring several books to a satisfying close, motivated them to read additional series, and fostered social energy.

5th Grade Readers:
Remember to submit questions for Friday's virtual author visit with Meg Medina and R. J. Palacio on the form in Google Classroom!

To celebrate their students' enthrallment with *Wonder* and *Merci Suárez Changes Gears*, fifth-grade teachers at Mamaroneck Avenue School hosted a virtual author visit with R. J. Palacio and Meg Medina.

For students who require the highest level of support

If your kidwatching and/or conferring reveal...	You might...
• the child is craving social connection related to the book	• connect the child with someone else who has read and enjoyed the book.

If you find yourself returning to this instructional option frequently, you should rethink the conditions for all children to read voluminously by...

- recognizing the myriad ways you respond, or don't respond, when you finish a book. Discuss your habits with students in mini-lessons so they can apply what is useful to them.
- instituting booktalks as a routine.
- celebrating books read at the end of each week by having students engage in booktalks and/or adding to a "Books We've Read This Year" chart.

See page 27 for details on these practices.

NEXT STEP

After the child has brought the reading experience to a close, return to the Volume Decision Tree on page 73 to answer **Diagnostic Question 7: Does the Child Have an Idea for a Next-Up Book?**

Does the Child Have an Idea for a Next-Up Book?

Why Is This Important?

Finishing a compelling book is cause for celebration. But it doesn't mean that our work is done. Now that the child has a successful reading experience behind her, it is critical to keep the momentum going. This is especially true for striving readers, who are vulnerable to stalls in their reading lives when they are between books.

Kidwatch

Observing a child when she is ready for a new reading experience gives you insights into her ability to propel her own reading life. Be on the lookout for agentive behavior to determine what the student already knows about finding a Next-Up book and what you can teach her.

As you kidwatch, ask yourself:

- Does the child keep a Next-Up Book List?
- After booktalks, does the child mention and/or write down titles she would like to read?
- Does the child make efforts to find Next-Up books (e.g., exploring book displays in the classroom/school library, seeking recommendations from peers, looking at book lists posted in the classroom)?
- Does the child know how to use digital tools to find Next-Up books?

Consider using online resources such as Padlet to keep track of books students want to read. Nathan uses the Padlet above as a Next-Up Book List. Once he has read the book, he moves the cover art to the "Books I've Finished" or "Books I Tried but Weren't For Me" columns, which serve as his book log.

Confer

Inquire into the child's go-to strategies for selecting a Next-Up book and her plan for reading beyond that book.

How do you usually decide what to read next? This will give you insight into what strategies, if any, the student has for finding a Next-Up book.

Now that you've finished your book, what do you plan to read next? A student may not yet have thought ahead to her next book. We want to teach students to develop that habit.

Are you interested in another book with similar content or themes? It can be easier for striving students to think broadly about their Next-Up books, rather than having to name a specific title. You can then help them narrow down their choices with a Preview Stack.

RELATED READINGS

- Gambrell, L. (1996). Creating classroom cultures that foster reading motivation. *The Reading Teacher (50)*1, 14–25.

- Krashen, S. (2011). *Free voluntary reading*. Libraries Unlimited.

- Shaffer, R., Cruser, B., Lowery, R. M., & Shults, L. (2019). Statement on independent reading. National Council of Teachers of English.

Is the book you just finished part of a series? Are you interested in continuing with the series? Reading through a series is an easy way to choose a Next-Up book and to accrue volume.

Did you enjoy the way this book was written? Would you like to try another book by the same author? By suggesting this to a student, you are teaching the student that she can find Next-Up books by searching for titles by a particular author.

Consider

If the child is interested in rereading the book, resist the urge to move her into something new. Instead, inquire about her reasons and recognize the value of repeated readings. See page 172 for details.

Collect/Track/Document

- Photos of Next-Up Book Lists
- Photos of a child's "yes" pile from a Preview Stack conference
- Screenshots of library book reservations

After finishing the Secret Coders series, Cooper left a note for his teacher requesting help finding a similar series, evidence of his developing agency and understanding of the people who can help him find great books.

DECISION TIME
Considering what you've learned, do you think the child has an idea for a Next-Up book?

YES

If yes, return to the Volume Decision Tree on page 72 and answer **Diagnostic Question 2: Can the Child Procure a Copy of the Selected Book?**

NO

If no, turn to page 76 for **Instructional Option 1: Guide the Child to Select a Book**.

Part III

TEACH: Responsive Practices

In Part III, we show you practical ways to teach your students about the importance of reading volume, and how to build their reading volume. Adding volume-related goals to your instructional repertoire and to students' intervention plans will complement instruction already in place and propel children along the virtuous cycle described in Chapter 1.

▶ Visit **scholastic.com/ReinventionResources** for downloadable forms, videos with the authors, and more!

Give an Interest Inventory to Learn the Child's Preferences

VOLUME-BUILDING FOCUS
- Choice
- Agency

GOAL
- To learn about students' reading preferences

YOU MIGHT TRY THIS IF...
- you don't know much about the child or his reading preferences.
- the child is no longer interested in books he used to enjoy.

GROUP SIZE
- One-on-one
- Small group
- Whole class

Completing an Interest Inventory helps students understand and define their reading preferences, which provides a window for you into their reading lives.

PREPARATION

- Print out a copy of the Interest Inventory for each student at scholastic.com/ReinventionResources.

STEPS

- To connect the Interest Inventory to book choice, you might say, *It's so important that we are able to choose the books that interest us and that we want to read. To help you find and choose books that you are excited to read, I am inviting you to complete this Interest Inventory.*

- Briefly review the Interest Inventory with the students.

- Allow students time to independently complete the Interest Inventory.

- Confer with students to offer support, clarify language, or answer questions as needed.

scholastic.com/ReinventionResources

NEXT STEP

Turn to page 111 to learn how to do a **Getting-to-Know-You Preview Stack**, using the student's Interest Inventory to help you select books.

Offer a Getting-to-Know-You Preview Stack

Engaging in a conversation about a stack of books you have hand-selected for the child allows you to gain valuable insights into their reading preferences. The child will likely walk away with compelling books to read, and furthermore, you will gain valuable information to make more targeted recommendations in the future.

PREPARATION

- Put together a stack of about ten books that you know the student can likely read with success.

- Aim for variety in genre, format, topic, font size, amount of print, frequency of illustration, and physical size.

- Print copies of the Prompting Guide and Notes Form for Preview and Review Stacks at scholastic.com/ReinventionResources.

scholastic.com/
ReinventionResources

STEPS

- Say to the student, *I picked out some books that I would like to look through with you. This will help us both understand your reading tastes. You may also find some books you would like to add to your book box for independent reading.*

- Spread the books in front of the student and ask, *Are there any books here that you know right away you would like to read? Are there any books here that you really are not interested in?*

- If the student is unsure, select a book from the pile and tell them a bit about it.

- Let them flip through various books in the stack, then encourage them to put the books into yes, no, or maybe piles.

- As the conference unfolds, use language from the Prompting Guide to elicit details about the student's interests and preferences.

- Remain neutral and validate the student's preferences, whether they like each book or not.

- Jot down observations and quotes on the Notes Form.

TIP

- Use what you've learned about the student's interests and preferences to inform future book recommendations.

VOLUME-BUILDING FOCUS
- Access
- Choice

GOALS
- To learn about the student's reading preferences
- To find a book for the student to read

YOU MIGHT TRY THIS IF...
- you don't know much about the child or their reading preferences.

GROUP SIZE
- One-on-one

SAMPLE GETTING-TO-KNOW-YOU PREVIEW STACK

Points to Consider

Amount of Text and Number of Illustrations per Page

Navigational Choices

Topics

Genres and Formats

NEXT STEPS

Did your Getting-to-Know-You Preview Stack conference help you to successfully guide the child to select a book?

Yes, and the child left the Getting-to-Know-You Preview Stack conference with a book in their hands.

Give them time to read some of the book, then return to the Volume Decision Tree on page 72 and answer **Diagnostic Question 3: Is the Child Invested in the Book?**

Yes, the Getting-to-Know-You Preview Stack helped you to recommend a title to the student, but they did not leave the conference with the actual book in their hands.

Return to the Volume Decision Tree on page 72 and answer **Diagnostic Question 2: Can the Child Procure a Copy of the Selected Book?**

Not yet, but you are getting to know this reader. Conduct another **Getting-to-Know-You Preview Stack** conference tomorrow with a new selection of books based on the information you have acquired.

Offer a Review Stack

A Review Stack conference helps the student build a reading identity by reminding her of previous reading successes and encouraging her to reflect on topics, genres, and features that appeal to her as a reader.

PREPARATION

- Gather a few books the student has engaged with recently.
- Include texts that the student enjoyed, as well as those she abandoned or read slowly.
- Print copies of the Prompting Guide and Notes Form at scholastic.com/ReinventionResources.

STEPS

- Spread the books in front of the student.
- Say to the student, *I've pulled together a pile of some of the books you've read this year. I'd like to look through them with you to help us both understand how you have evolved as a reader. Are there any that you would like to talk about first—maybe one that you really enjoyed or one that you really did not like? Was there anything going on that influenced your experience with the book? For example, maybe a friend recommended it, or you read it during vacation.*
- Use the Prompting Guide to ask questions and determine the student's preferences.
- Remain neutral and validate her comments and preferences, whether she likes the book or not.
- Take notes on the Notes Form as the conference unfolds. You might take a picture of the stack against a white background before the conference and annotate the photo.

scholastic.com/
ReinventionResources

VOLUME-BUILDING FOCUS

- Agency

GOAL

- To explore the student's reading history to understand her reading preferences

YOU MIGHT TRY THIS IF...

- you have done several Preview Stacks and are still having trouble matching the student with a book.
- the child frequently abandons books.
- the child would benefit from exploring how her reading choices have evolved over time.
- the child has been reading the same topic, genre, format, author, or series for a long time.

GROUP SIZE

- One-on-one

TIPS

- Don't lose sight of the fact that striving readers are frequently labeled as "serial abandoners." Think of times in your own reading history when you abandoned books. That will help you empathize as you work with the student to consider her reading preferences and experiences.
- Acknowledge that there are valid reasons for abandoning books. Support the student by providing (1) books that offer navigational choice such as expository nonfiction and (2) short texts while continuing to gradually expose the student to longer texts.

Hot Dog/Press Start

✓ illustrations

✓ large font

✓ white space

Who Would Win?

✓ dangerous animals

✓ nonfiction

"I like to guess who's going to win. Usually, I'm right."

I Survived

✓ action-packed

"I like to imagine what I would do."

Enjoyed the graphic versions.

✗ too many words in traditional format

Surviving in the Wild

✓ nonlinear structure

✓ survival

Returned to this book several times this year.

Captain Underpants

✓ likes the movie

✓ silly humor

✗ too much text

"The words are hard."

This copy has been in his book box all year.

Dog Man

✓ graphic format

Has read each book in the series many times.

Marvel Storybook

✓ short stories

✓ illustrations

✓ super heroes

Next steps

- Try more series with short chapters, illustrations, and white space.
- Introduce more nonfiction.
- Continue encouraging graphic novels.

NEXT STEPS

Reflect on what the student has told you to make a plan.

If you think the child is interested in trying one of the books in the Review Stack again, give her time to read some of it, then return to the Volume Decision Tree on page 72 and answer **Diagnostic Question 3: Is the Child Invested in the Book?**

If you think the student would benefit from support in finding engaging texts, you might use the knowledge you gained from the Review Stack conference to conduct a **Jump-Start Preview Stack.** See page 115 for details.

Offer a Jump-Start Preview Stack

Jump-Start Preview Stack conferences invite students to reflect on how their reading preferences have evolved and encourage them to select texts they are eager to read. They are a great way to help children regain reading momentum when their reading lives have stalled because they just aren't that into the books they've been choosing.

PREPARATION

- Using notes from previous conferences, reflect on what you know about the student's interests and reading preferences.

- Put together a stack of six to ten books that vary in topic, genre, format, and elements of kid appeal. Be sure that they are books that the student can read comfortably—the goal is to set him up for a successful reading experience.

- Print copies of the Prompting Guide and Notes Form at scholastic.com/ ReinventionResources.

scholastic.com/
ReinventionResources

VOLUME-BUILDING FOCUS
- Access
- Choice

GOALS
- To understand the student's current reading preferences
- To match the student with books

YOU MIGHT TRY THIS IF...
- a student is experiencing a lull in his reading volume and needs inspiration.

GROUP SIZE
- One-on-one

STEPS

- Spread the books in front of the student and say, *I've pulled together a pile of books that I think you might like. I'd like to look through them with you to see if we can find some books that you are excited to read. Take a look through the stack to see if there are any that look interesting, and I'll tell you why I picked them for you.*

- As you make your way through the stack with the student, share the reasons why you selected various titles. *I picked* The Dog: Best in Show *for you because I know that you have a new puppy at home, and I've noticed that you enjoy reading nonfiction books like the* Who Would Win? *series. Is there anything you like or dislike about this book? Are you interested in reading about dogs?*

- Remain neutral and validate the student's preferences, whether he likes the book or not. Jot observations and comments on the recording form.

- Encourage the child to put books into yes, no, or maybe piles.

- As the conference unfolds, use language from the Prompting Guide to elicit details about the student's interests and preferences. Jot down observations and quotes on the Notes Form.

TIPS

- Keep in mind, not every book in the stack needs to be a new read. You might encourage the student to reread an old favorite to regain momentum.

- Inquire about other reasons the child has lost momentum. Verify that he has a quiet spot and enough time to read each day. Investigate other factors that might be inhibiting reading volume.

ALEX'S JUMP-START PREVIEW STACK

Alex is into his personal style. He might enjoy this rhythmic picture book.

Because Alex has enjoyed several graphic novels, he may enjoy this series as well.

Alex has a new dog at home and seems to enjoy nonfiction.

Given his love for animals, Alex might like this illustrated series.

Each book was selected based on conversations with Alex and findings from the Review Stack conference with him. Most are quick reads designed to give Alex positive and successful experiences to help him gain momentum in his reading life.

Some of Alex's friends are into this series, and he might enjoy it, too.

Because he prefers lots of white space, Alex might enjoy a novel in verse.

NEXT STEPS

Did your Jump-Start Preview Stack conference help you to guide the child to select a book?

Yes, and the child left the conference with a book in his hands. Give him some time to read some of the book, and then return to the Volume Decision Tree on page 72 to answer **Diagnostic Question 3: Is the Child Invested in the Book?**

Yes, the conference helped you to recommend a title to the child, but he did not leave with the book in his hands. Return to the Volume Decision Tree on page 72 and answer **Diagnostic Question 2: Can the Child Procure a Copy of the Selected Book?**

Not yet, but you are getting to know the child as a reader. Conduct another **Jump-Start Preview Stack** conference tomorrow with a new selection of books based on the information you have acquired.

Offer a Gentle-Nudge Preview Stack

In this conference, the student considers whether they are ready to begin exploring new reading territory by trying new genres, formats, topics, or levels of sophistication. Gentle-Nudge Preview Stacks are a non-threatening way to expose a student to texts they might enjoy but are unlikely to pick up on their own.

PREPARATION

- Put together a stack of six to ten books. Be sure that they are books that the student can read comfortably—the goal is to set them up for a successful reading experience.

- Include books that relate in some way to texts the student has enjoyed in the past (e.g., a topic of interest but in a new format, a preferred format but a new genre).

- Include a few completely unrelated titles that you think the student might enjoy.

- Print copies of the Prompting Guide and Notes Form at scholastic.com/ReinventionResources.

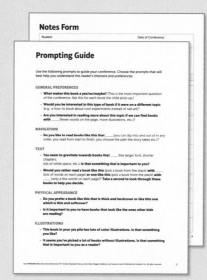

scholastic.com/
ReinventionResources

STEPS

- Spread the books in front of the student and say, *I've noticed that you have been reading a lot of graphic novels recently. It is wonderful that you have found a format that grabs you as a reader! I wanted to show you a few books that I think you might also enjoy. Are there any books here that look interesting or not so interesting?*

- Explain why you selected the books. *I've noticed that many of the graphic novels you have read are fantasies, so I thought you might enjoy this fantasy novel. It has a lot of white space on the page and short chapters, which I like since that helps me to move through the book quickly.*

- Let them flip through various books in the stack, then encourage them to put the books into yes, no, or maybe piles.

- As the conference unfolds, use language from the Prompting Guide to elicit details about the student's interests and preferences.

- Jot down observations and quotes on the Notes Form.

VOLUME-BUILDING FOCUS

- Access
- Choice

GOAL

- To expose the student to genres, formats, topics, or levels of sophistication that they have not experienced recently

YOU MIGHT TRY THIS IF...

- the child tends to stay within their reading comfort zone, even though they seem ready to take on different or more challenging texts.

- you think the child is ready to explore new topics, genres, formats, authors, or series

GROUP SIZE

- One-on-one

- Adopt a non-judgmental inquiry stance when exploring a student's reading experiences. Learn about the benefits of lingering in comfortable or familiar books on page 123.

- Remain patient if the student doesn't choose any of the books in the stack. It may take weeks before he is ready to move on from a beloved series, format, genre, or topic.

- Avoid using this practice with students who are reading voluminously.

RICHIE'S GENTLE-NUDGE STACK

The books in this stack were selected for Richie, a child who has been reading graphic novels and may be ready for a new format.

Dog Man has been a favorite series for Richie in recent weeks. This series served as a jumping-off point for selecting the following books for Richie's Gentle-Nudge stack.

Richie might enjoy another series by Dav Pilkey. The fast-paced storyline will support him in taking longer stretches of text.

The mix of facts, jokes, and photographs may keep Richie's interest in this nonfiction selection.

Since Richie has read the I Survived graphic novels, he might be ready to try the narrative version.

This collection of biographies may appeal to Richie since each profile is only one page, and he can dip in and out of the book in any order.

Richie loves horror movies. He may enjoy this highly illustrated series of scary stories with plenty of white space on each page.

NEXT STEPS

Did your Gentle-Nudge Preview Stack conference help you to successfully guide the child to select a book?

Yes, and the child left with a book. Provide time for the child to read some of the book, then return to the Volume Decision Tree on page 72 to answer **Diagnostic Question 3: Is the Child Invested in the Book?**

Yes, and the child left with a recommendation, but does not have the book. Return to the Volume Decision Tree on page 72 and answer **Diagnostic Question 2: Can the Child Procure a Copy of the Selected Book?**

Not yet, but you are getting to know this reader. Conduct another **Gentle-Nudge Preview Stack** conference tomorrow with a new selection of books based on the information you have acquired.

Urge Reading Partners to Make Recommendations

Learning the art of recommending books helps children develop readerly habits and fosters social energy around favorite titles. Students also come to recognize that fellow readers are valuable resources for pinpointing Next-Up Books.

PREPARATION

- Ask students to choose a book that they have recently read and would like to recommend to another reader.
- Pair readers with similar reading capabilities.
- Select a book you have recently read to model making a book recommendation.

STEPS

- Gather students with their chosen books and say, *An important part of our reading lives is sharing the books that we've loved with other readers. Asking friends for book recommendations can also be a great way to find books to read.*
- Prompt students to do some thinking. *We each have a book with us that we have enjoyed and want to recommend. Before making our recommendations, we are going to think about three things: 1) What was this book about? 2) What did I like about it? 3) How did this book touch my mind and heart or spark my imagination?*
- Model how to give a brief summary of the plot without revealing any spoilers. For example, *I just finished reading* I Survived the Sinking of the Titanic, 1912 *by Lauren Tarshis. It's an adventure story about a boy named George who is passing his time during the voyage by exploring all of the exciting parts of the ship. One day, while he's in the first-class storage cabin, the boat shakes violently. Suddenly, George needs to figure out how to stay alive as the ship begins to sink.*
- Think aloud to help students determine what they like about a book. *When you reflect on what you like about the book, you can think about the genre, format, plot, writing style, or special features. I really liked the action-packed, fast pace of this book and the short chapters. The author kept me in suspense, and I couldn't wait to see what would happen next!*
- Think aloud to help them discover how a book made them think or touched them emotionally. *When making a recommendation, it's also important to think about how this book touched your mind and your heart. What did it make you think about? How did it make you feel?* I Survived the Sinking of the Titanic *made me think about what I would do in the same situation. Would I be brave? Resourceful? It made me feel grateful*

VOLUME-BUILDING FOCUS

- Access
- Choice
- Agency

GOALS

- To access and choose books through partner recommendations
- To articulate and share your reading preferences
- To build social energy around reading

YOU MIGHT TRY THIS IF...

- another child in the class has similar reading capabilities and interests, and may be able to help in finding a Next-Up Book.
- social energy is building around a particular book, series, or topic, but the child has not yet been affected by it.

GROUP SIZE

- Small group
- Whole class

for all I have in my life because you never know when you might find yourself in an unexpected situation.

- Give students time to think and prepare. *Take a few minutes now to think about why you want to recommend the book in front of you. What was the book about? What did you like about the book? How did the book touch your mind and/or pique your curiosity?* As students think, you can confer with them and help them focus their summaries and articulate their preferences.

- Bring partners together and have them take turns recommending their books to each other.

TIP

- Try pairing or grouping students who are reading similarly accessible/complex books to increase the likelihood that each of them will be well matched with a book that they can read with high success.

When Recommending a Book
Ask Yourself:

① What did I like about the book?
- genre
- format
- plot
- author's writing style

② Did this book give me something to think and talk about?

③ How did this book touch my mind and my heart?

NEXT STEP

Encourage the student to use partner recommendations to find a book she wants to read. Once she has selected a book, return to the Volume Decision Tree on page 72 and answer
Diagnostic Question 2: Can the Child Procure a Copy of the Selected Book?

Create Next-Up Book Lists

Next-Up Book Lists are an easy way for readers to keep track of books they want to read, saving them time when they are ready to choose their next read. Next-Up Book Lists can also be used as a tool to help students identify their reading preferences.

STEPS

- Frame the purpose of creating a Next-Up Book List by saying, *As a community of readers, we are always talking about books, making recommendations to each other, and sharing titles that we love. It's a good idea to keep track of the many books that interest us and that we may want to read in the future. One way to do this is to make a Next-Up Book List.*

- Share your own Next-Up Book List. *This is my list. On the left side, I list the titles of the books that interest me. On the right side, I keep notes about the book to help me remember why I put it on my list. I write down where I saw the book, who recommended it to me, or when I think I might read it. For example, I am interested in reading a nonfiction book called* Thinking Fast and Slow. *My brother recommended this book to me, so I wrote that in my notes section. That way, if I decide to read this book, I can talk to my brother about the book, or even ask to borrow his copy.*

- Model how to begin a Next-Up Book List. *Turn to the back of your reading notebook. Now make a T-chart. Label the left side "Titles" and/or "Authors," and the right side "Notes."*

- Give students time to add some books to their lists. *Take a few minutes right now to add a book or two to your list that you are interested in reading. It might be a book that was featured in a class booktalk, a recommendation from a friend, or the next book in a series. You can also add any important notes about the book.*

- Remind students that the list is ongoing. *You can keep adding to your Next-Up Book List any time you find a book that appeals to you and that you may want to read.*

- When you complete a book of your own, model how you use your Next-Up Book List to consider possibilities and choose your next read.

VOLUME-BUILDING FOCUS
- Access
- Choice

GOAL
- To help students to develop the habit of recording books that they find engaging

YOU MIGHT TRY THIS IF...
- the child is ready to find books on his own but still over-relies on you for help.
- the child does not have reliable resources to find Next-Up Books.

GROUP SIZE
- One-on-one
- Small group
- Whole class

Name: Dylan	
I am currently reading:	**Books on Deck:**
~~Kingdom of Wrenly #1~~ 107 pages	Kingdom of Wrenly #9
~~Kingdom of Wrenly #2~~ 109 pages	run away dolls,
~~Kingdom of Wrenly #3~~ 115	Kingdom of wrenly #10
~~Kingdom of Wrenly #4~~ 115	~~Flying beaver brothers #1~~ 9
~~Kingdom of Wrenly #5~~ 117	Flying beaver brothers #2
Kingdom of wrenly #6	Flying beaver brothers #3
Kingdom of wrenly #8	Flying beaver brothers #4
	Flying beaver brothers #5

Third-grade teacher Liz Johnson encourages students to tape their Next-Up Book List to their book box so that it's always close by.

TIPS

- If it seems appropriate to do so, have students create digital versions of Next-Up Book Lists on platforms such as Padlet. These can double as reading logs if students move books they have completed or abandoned into separate columns.

- Don't be surprised if students need regular reminders to add to their Next-Up Book Lists before doing so becomes a habit.

NEXT STEP

Remind the student to consult his Next-Up Book List to find books he wants to read. Once he has selected a book, return to the Volume Decision Tree on page 72 and answer **Diagnostic Question 2: Can the Child Procure a Copy of the Selected Book?**

Explore the Benefits of Lingering in Comfortable or Familiar Books

Teachers and parents are often eager to nudge students into longer, harder books or out of specific formats such as graphic or expository texts. Sometimes that is just what a student needs, but sometimes it is counterproductive. Being allowed to linger in a favorite series, dive more deeply into a specific topic, or spend time with a beloved author is often the best prescription for reading success. When we understand the benefits of dwelling in a desired text, topic, or format (an experience Stephen Krashen calls "narrow reading"), we can help children make decisions about when it is best to linger and when it is time to move on.

PREPARATION

- Post chart paper to create a Benefits of Dwelling anchor chart.

STEPS

- Introduce the students to the concept of dwelling in a text or topic by giving examples from your own reading life. *There have been times when I have stayed with a series or topic for a really long time. A few years ago, my mother-in-law introduced me to the Outlander series by Diana Gabaldon. It took me close to a year to make my way through the entire series. My husband thought I was crazy for sticking with the books for so long, but I was so interested and invested in the story that I just couldn't move on.*

- Encourage students to think back to a similar experience from their own reading lives and have them brainstorm some of the benefits they got out of the experience.

- Co-construct an anchor chart highlighting benefits of "dwelling," which may include...

  ▸ Learning new vocabulary more easily

  ▸ Understanding the story or topic more deeply or in new ways

  ▸ Remaining motivated to read voluminously

  ▸ Feeling immersed in the world of the story

  ▸ Enjoying a familiar, comfortable reading experience

  ▸ Becoming better prepared to read more challenging texts when the time is right

- Support students in making informed decisions about when the time is right to dwell in a text or topic. *When you find yourself returning to the same book, series, topic, or format over and over again, think about whether you are getting some of these benefits out of the experience or whether you may be ready to move on to something new.*

VOLUME-BUILDING FOCUS
- Choice
- Agency

GOAL
- To understand when it is productive to linger in a book, series, format, or topic

YOU MIGHT TRY THIS IF...
- the student is engrossed in a series.
- the student reads the same books over and over again.
- the student is reading almost exclusively books from a specific topic, genre, or author.

GROUP SIZE
- One-on-one
- Small group
- Whole class

TIPS

- If several months of dwelling in a similar text, topic, or format seems like a long time, consider how it will be remembered by the student as they reflect on their reading life years down the road. For example, when Annie was in fifth grade, she read Patricia Clapp's historical fiction novel *Constance* so many times that she can still visualize the feisty title character's first kiss in snowy Plymouth.

- Consider sharing the benefits of dwelling in text with parents, especially those who may be in a hurry for their children to read more challenging books.

Benefits of Lingering

When we linger in favorite series, pore over formats we love, or spend time with authors and topics that excite us, we can:

- learn new **vocabulary** more easily
- stay motivated to **read voluminously**
- **understand** the story/topic in new ways
- more deeply comprehend **literary devices**
- feel **immersed** in the world of the story
- **enjoy** a comfortable, familiar experience
- become **prepared** to take on more challenging texts when the time is right

NEXT STEPS

If you and the student determine that dwelling in a text is beneficial at this point, encourage them to continue on this reading path.

If you and the student determine that lingering with their current selection is best, give them time to read some of the book, then return to the Volume Decision Tree on page 72 and answer **Diagnostic Question 3: Is the Child Invested in the Book?**

If you and the student determine that they are ready to try something new, turn to page 117 to conduct a **Gentle-Nudge Preview Stack** conference.

Explore the Benefits of Branching Out Into New Reading Territory

"Reading ladders," a concept first introduced by the National Council of Teachers of English in 1947 and refined by Teri Lesesne (2010), refers to moving students incrementally into more complex or challenging texts over time. This practice affords children opportunities to grow as readers and gain exposure to authors, genres, formats, and topics they may not have otherwise discovered while maintaining a flow of high-success reading. When you sense that a child is ready, help them to embark on new reading adventures.

PREPARATION

- Post chart paper to create an Is It Time to Start Something New? anchor chart.

STEPS

- Introduce the students to the concept of reading ladders by giving examples from your own reading life. *When I was in sixth grade, I read just about every historical fiction book in my school library. Everyone knew me as the historical fiction kid. I loved those books, but my school librarian suspected that I might also enjoy books from other genres. She recommended some nonfiction books from the history section, a few adventure novels, and even a couple of sci-fi stories. Guess what? I never lost my love of historical fiction, but I realized that there were lots of other kinds of books out there that I also enjoyed.*

- Encourage students to think back to a time when they ventured into new reading territory. Have them brainstorm some of the benefits they got out of the experience (e.g., discovered they loved a format they had never before tried, realized that they enjoyed the challenge of reading an entirely new genre).

- Co-construct an anchor chart identifying when it might be time to move into new or more challenging reading territory. This might include:

  - ▸ You're growing bored of the books you've been reading.

  - ▸ You return to the same books because you're not sure what else to read.

  - ▸ You aren't sure where or how to find different books.

  - ▸ You're ready to take on a reading challenge.

  - ▸ You're interested in reading something completely (or just a little!) different.

- Support students in making informed decisions about when the time is right to move along a reading ladder. *When you find yourself returning to the same book, series, topic, or format over and*

VOLUME-BUILDING FOCUS
- Choice
- Agency

GOAL
- To nudge the student into reading experiences that may be new or slightly more challenging

YOU MIGHT TRY THIS IF...
- you suspect the student is ready to take on a new challenge or have a new reading experience.
- they are growing tired of familiar reads.

GROUP SIZE
- One-on-one
- Small group
- Whole class

It Might Be Time to Try Something New

- If you return to the same book(s) because you're not sure **what else** to read
- If you don't know **where** or **how** to find new or different books
- If you're growing **bored** with the books you've been reading
- You're ready to try something **different**
- If you're interested in taking on a reading **challenge**

over again, *think about whether you may be ready to move on to something new.*

- Keep in mind, just as a person climbing a ladder keeps one foot on a familiar rung as he steps upward with the other, a reader benefits from books that contain some familiar elements as he steps incrementally into new territory.

TIPS

- Avoid moving students along prematurely. Read about the benefits of dwelling in texts, topics, and themes on page 123.
- Move gently up the reading ladder with vulnerable readers being careful to never put them in a position of facing texts that are much too hard.

RELATED READING

Lesesne, T. S. (2010). *Reading ladders: Leading students from where they are to where we'd like them to be.* Heinemann.

NEXT STEPS

Choose one of these directions.

If you and the student determine that lingering with their current selection is best, give them time to read some of the book, then return to the Volume Decision Tree on page 72 and answer **Diagnostic Question 3: Is the Child Invested in the Book?**

If you and the student determine that they are ready to try something new, turn to page 117 to conduct a **Gentle-Nudge Preview Stack** conference.

Take an Inquiry Tour of the Classroom Library

An inquiry tour is perfect for readers who feel overwhelmed by the choices in the classroom or have difficulty choosing books on their own. Taking an inquiry tour builds students' familiarity with the collection and teaches them strategies for selecting Next-Up Books.

PREPARATION

- Observe the student shop from the classroom library prior to this practice. Take note of the following:
- How much time does the student take to choose a book?
- How many baskets/sections of the library does he explore?
- Does he seem to meaningfully consider books, or to make more random choices?

STEPS

- Provide a rationale for the practice. *I've noticed that sometimes it feels challenging for you to find books that you really want to read in our classroom library. Today I thought we could explore the library together so you can get to know our collection better.*

- Ask the student to pick out a basket that is very familiar to him, a "go-to" basket that he often chooses books from. Take a few minutes to discuss what he likes about these books (e.g., a beloved series, a preferred format, books that feel comfortable to read).

- Ask him to choose a basket that looks interesting but feels unfamiliar. Explore this basket together. Provide support by giving an overview of the contents. For example, *This basket has biographies, which are the stories of people's lives.* Where possible, point out features that the student has enjoyed in other books. *This one has an illustrated timeline, just like the one in the dinosaur book you were reading last week.* Ask the student whether he would like to try reading any of the books in the basket.

- Encourage the student to continue to explore at least one unfamiliar basket each time he visits the classroom library to continue to broaden his knowledge of available books.

VOLUME-BUILDING FOCUS
- Access
- Choice
- Agency

GOAL
- To build the student's knowledge of the classroom library and empower him to self-select books

YOU MIGHT TRY THIS IF...
- your classroom library has books the child wants to read and can read, but he has trouble finding those books.

GROUP SIZE
- One-on-one
- Small group
- Whole class

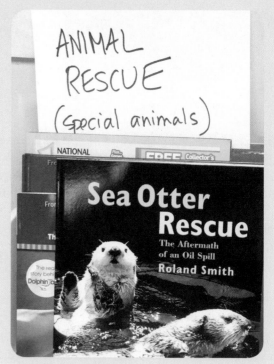

TIPS

- Don't feel compelled to introduce the student to the entire library in one visit. You can tour the library together over several days, exploring a few baskets at a time.

- Curate your classroom library so that it is filled with books at your students' independent reading levels and contains a variety of topics, formats, and genres. See Chapter 2 and "The Leaky Faucet Case Study" in *From Striving to Thriving: How to Grow Confident, Capable Readers* (Harvey & Ward, 2007).

NEXT STEP

As the student becomes comfortable navigating the classroom library, reinforce the idea that he can find books he wants to read from those shelves. Once he has selected a book to read, give him time to read some of the book. Then, return to the Volume Decision Tree on page 72 and answer **Diagnostic Question 3: Is the Child Invested in the Book?**

Use Book Maps to Explore Reading Interests

This is an adaptation of Nancie Atwell's Reading Territories from *In the Middle* (2014). Using a book or series the child enjoyed reading in the past for inspiration, have them brainstorm various elements that grabbed their attention. The goal is for students to understand and articulate their interests and preferences, like the eighth grader who asked librarian Kelsey Cohen for "a graphic memoir with a little edge like *Hey Kiddo* or *Stitches*."

PREPARATION

- Select a book you have read aloud to the class.
- Ask students to find a book they enjoyed reading in the past.
- Print copies of the Book Map at scholastic.com/ReinventionResources.

STEPS

- Say to the student(s), *Readers are always on the lookout for their next great read. One way to make this easier is to take a close look at a book we enjoyed reading in the past to figure out what it is about that book that really grabbed our attention. Today, I want to show you one way you can do this—book mapping. My Book Map is going to be based on one of my favorite series, The Bad Guys, so I'll write "The Bad Guys" in the middle.*

- Go through each category, modeling how to select features that made that book particularly appealing and adding them to the Book Map. *As I flip through* The Bad Guys, *I notice that the chapters are short and there is just a little bit of text on each page. Now that I think of it, I really like books that have short chapters; it makes me feel like I'm accomplishing something as I read chapter after chapter. On my Book Map, I'm going to go to the Inside of the Book section and put a star next to "Short Chapters," since that is really important to me. I'm also going to put a checkmark next to "Just a Little Text on Each Page," since that's something I like, but it's not as important as chapter length.* Continue modeling how to fill out the Book Map with a few more categories.

- Say to the student(s), *Now look through your book and use the Book Map categories to help you fill in your Book Map.*

- Encourage students to use their Book Map to help them choose Next-Up Books and to use it as a tool when seeking recommendations. Perhaps coordinate with the librarian to find times when students can visit with their Book Maps for helping in finding Next-Up Books.

VOLUME-BUILDING FOCUS
- Choice
- Agency

GOALS
- To pinpoint the specific ideas, themes, or features that grab students as readers
- To provide students "book language" for describing the topics, themes, and features that grab them (e.g., format, kid appeal, white space, plot, theme, etc.)

YOU MIGHT TRY THIS IF...
- the child recently finished a book or series that they enjoyed and is having difficulty selecting a Next-Up Book.
- the child has difficulty articulating their reading preferences.

GROUP SIZE
- One-on-one
- Small group
- Whole class

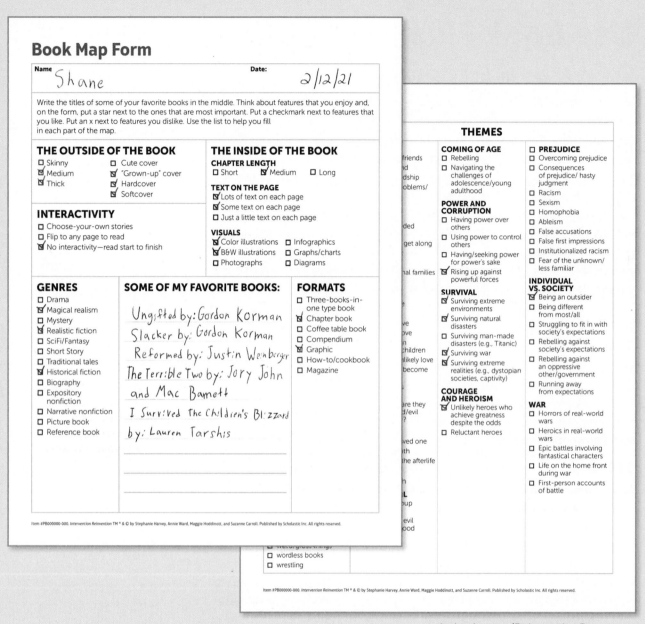

Book Map Form

Name Shane

Date: 2/12/21

Write the titles of some of your favorite books in the middle. Think about features that you enjoy and, on the form, put a star next to the ones that are most important. Put a checkmark next to features that you like. Put an x next to features you dislike. Use the list to help you fill in each part of the map.

THE OUTSIDE OF THE BOOK
- ☐ Skinny
- ☑ Medium
- ☑ Thick
- ☐ Cute cover
- ☑ "Grown-up" cover
- ☑ Hardcover
- ☑ Softcover

INTERACTIVITY
- ☐ Choose-your-own stories
- ☐ Flip to any page to read
- ☑ No interactivity—read start to finish

THE INSIDE OF THE BOOK
CHAPTER LENGTH
- ☐ Short
- ☑ Medium
- ☐ Long

TEXT ON THE PAGE
- ☑ Lots of text on each page
- ☑ Some text on each page
- ☐ Just a little text on each page

VISUALS
- ☑ Color illustrations
- ☑ B&W illustrations
- ☐ Photographs
- ☐ Infographics
- ☐ Graphs/charts
- ☐ Diagrams

GENRES
- ☐ Drama
- ☑ Magical realism
- ☐ Mystery
- ☑ Realistic fiction
- ☐ SciFi/Fantasy
- ☐ Short Story
- ☐ Traditional tales
- ☑ Historical fiction
- ☐ Biography
- ☐ Expository nonfiction
- ☐ Narrative nonfiction
- ☐ Picture book
- ☐ Reference book

SOME OF MY FAVORITE BOOKS:
Ungifted by: Gordon Korman
Slacker by: Gordon Korman
Reformed by: Justin Weinberger
The Terrible Two by: Jory John and Mac Barnett
I Survived The Children's Blizzard by: Lauren Tarshis

FORMATS
- ☐ Three-books-in-one type book
- ☑ Chapter book
- ☐ Coffee table book
- ☐ Compendium
- ☑ Graphic
- ☐ How-to/cookbook
- ☐ Magazine

Item #PB000000-000. *Intervention Reinvention* TM ® & © by Stephanie Harvey, Annie Ward, Maggie Hoddinott, and Suzanne Carroll. Published by Scholastic Inc. All rights reserved.

THEMES

COMING OF AGE
- ☐ Rebelling
- ☐ Navigating the challenges of adolescence/young adulthood

POWER AND CORRUPTION
- ☐ Having power over others
- ☐ Using power to control others
- ☐ Having/seeking power for power's sake
- ☑ Rising up against powerful forces

SURVIVAL
- ☑ Surviving extreme environments
- ☑ Surviving natural disasters
- ☑ Surviving man-made disasters (e.g., Titanic)
- ☑ Surviving war
- ☑ Surviving extreme realities (e.g., dystopian societies, captivity)

COURAGE AND HEROISM
- ☑ Unlikely heroes who achieve greatness despite the odds
- ☐ Reluctant heroes

☐ PREJUDICE
- ☐ Overcoming prejudice
- ☐ Consequences of prejudice/ hasty judgment
- ☐ Racism
- ☐ Sexism
- ☐ Homophobia
- ☐ Ableism
- ☐ False accusations
- ☐ False first impressions
- ☐ Institutionalized racism
- ☐ Fear of the unknown/ less familiar

INDIVIDUAL VS. SOCIETY
- ☑ Being an outsider
- ☐ Being different from most/all
- ☐ Struggling to fit in with society's expectations
- ☐ Rebelling against society's expectations
- ☐ Rebelling against an oppressive other/government
- ☐ Running away from expectations

WAR
- ☐ Horrors of real-world wars
- ☐ Heroics in real-world wars
- ☐ Epic battles involving fantastical characters
- ☐ Life on the home front during war
- ☐ First-person accounts of battle

- ☐ weird/gross things
- ☐ wordless books
- ☐ wrestling

Item #PB000000-000. *Intervention Reinvention* TM ® & © by Stephanie Harvey, Annie Ward, Maggie Hoddinott, and Suzanne Carroll. Published by Scholastic Inc. All rights reserved.

scholastic.com/ReinventionResources

TIP
- Consider pairing up students with similar interests to complete their reading maps together. They might be able to provide each other with specific title recommendations to add to their Next-Up Book Lists.

NEXT STEP
Encourage the student to use their Book Map to find books they want to read. Once they have selected a book, return to the Volume Decision Tree on page 72 and answer **Diagnostic Question 2: Can the Child Procure a Copy of the Selected Book?**

Intensify With "Book-Match Plus"

Inspired by curation services such as Stitch Fix, Book-Match Plus is one of the most intense interventions we've devised in which books are hand-selected and delivered to striving readers on a regular and ongoing basis. Too often, striving readers—the students who need the most abundant access to compelling, accessible texts—spend their days in book droughts with little or nothing to read. Book-Match Plus provides an opportunity for classroom teachers, librarians, and out-of-classroom specialists to collaborate to meet the needs of striving readers. An intervention like Book-Match Plus is particularly vital when individual readers' capabilities and interests are well outside the mainstream and cannot be matched with books in the classroom library.

PREPARATION

Print a copy of the Notes Form at scholastic.com/ReinventionResources. If the child has already completed an Interest Inventory, get a copy of it; otherwise print a copy from scholastic.com/ReinventionResources.

STEPS

Any member of the team: Sit with the student to explore her interests and reading preferences. Capture the student's preferences on the Interest Inventory in as much specific detail as possible (e.g., "gymnast Simone Biles" as opposed to "sports"). Share these with the book-matching partner.

scholastic.com/ReinventionResources

VOLUME-BUILDING FOCUS
- Access
- Choice

GOAL
- To provide your most vulnerable readers with access to accessible and highly appealing books

YOU MIGHT TRY THIS IF...
- a student in your class is reading well below the range of books you have available.

GROUP SIZE
- One-on-one

Book-matching partner (e.g., librarian, out-of-classroom specialist): Using the student's responses as a guide, identify six to ten highly appealing books that the student can read successfully. Ideally, these will be on hand in the school library, public library, or other classrooms. If not, see our tip about ordering books for striving readers with niche interests. It is crucial that the books have an air of novelty and cachet; not just any books will do! Your most vulnerable strivers may be receptive only to books in narrow interest bands, necessitating painstaking sourcing. Box the books up and deliver them to the classroom.

Classroom teacher:
- Follow the procedures for Offer a Getting-to-Know-You Preview Stack on page 111.
- Capture the student's responses on the Notes Form.
- Encourage the student to keep the books she put in the yes pile and begin reading them.

- Put the books from the no pile and the Notes Form in the box.
- Return the box to the book-matching partner so she can begin sourcing books for the next box based on the Notes form.

Book-matching partner: Using information from the Notes Form and the student's Interest Inventory, curate a new set of books. Continue to track and respond to the child's evolving preferences and reading capabilities, curating Book-Match Plus boxes until the child is able to access books successfully on her own. To learn more about gains made by Mamaroneck readers through Book-Match Plus, see pages 57–59.

Together as a team: Monitor the child's reading progress looking for evidence that she is able to successfully access books on her own and is ready to "graduate" from Book-Match Plus. Note that she may need support learning how to successfully choose and procure appealing, high-success reads independently.

TIPS

- When working with striving readers, particularly those who have unique interests, it may be necessary to ask an administrator about placing niche orders. The books can be set aside in a special Book-Match Plus collection when a student has finished reading them. In Mamaroneck, we have come to recognize that the cost of Book-Match Plus books (typically less than 50 dollars per box) pales in comparison to the cost of workbooks or other intervention programs.

- If you find that your classroom library is not meeting the needs of the vast majority of your students, use the tools in Create and Curate Robust, Vibrant, and Diverse Classroom Libraries from 10 Foundational Actions (page 29) to help you curate your collection for the readers in your class.

- Given the intensity of this intervention, focus your efforts on your most striving readers. After all, thriving readers often have multiple access streams for new books, beginning with the classroom library.

NEXT STEPS

Did your Book-Match Plus efforts help you to successfully guide the child to select a book?

Yes, and the child left the Preview Stack conference with a book in her hands. Give her time to read some of the book, then return to the Volume Decision Tree on page 72 and answer **Diagnostic Question 3: Is the Child Invested in the Book?**

Not yet, but you are getting to know this reader. Curate a new Book-Match Plus collection based on the information you have acquired and conduct another **Preview Stack** conference tomorrow.

Give Booktalks to Build Social Energy Around Books

Booktalks are an efficient way to build enthusiasm for genres, formats, or topics students may know little about. They also provide an opportunity to highlight books of all types and levels, which fosters an inclusive reading community. Making a daily habit of highlighting texts through one-minute booktalks is ideal and becomes especially important when you notice that students are losing enthusiasm for reading.

STEPS

- Select a book that most students can read successfully. Be sure to regularly include titles that your most striving reader can read independently.

- Hold up the book and tell students the title, genre, and format. Point out any unique features (e.g., infographics, maps, short chapters). Provide a very short summary and/or read a few lines out loud. For example, *Today I wanted to share with you* The Bad Guys *by Aaron Blabey. This hilarious fantasy has lots of illustrations and just a few words on each page, so it's sure to be a page-turner. The main characters in the book are bad guys trying to be good, but their efforts lead to some hilarious situations. If you're a fan of Dog Man, this series would be a great Next-Up Book!*

- Leave the book in an accessible place along with a sign-up sheet for kids who want to read the book next.

- Keep a list of books that have been book-talked for students to refer to later.

TIPS

- Once you've done a handful of booktalks, gradually release responsibility to students by encouraging them to book-talk titles they think their peers will enjoy.

- Check out the trove of booktalks curated here: scholastic.com/teacher/ab/booktalks.htm

- Get quick synopses from book reviews and book summaries, available at websites such as Amazon and Titlewave.

- Share with students websites to access booktalks on their own, such as kids.scholastic.com/kids/videos/book-trailers.

VOLUME-BUILDING FOCUS

- Access
- Choice
- Agency

GOAL

- To introduce students to a variety of books

YOU MIGHT TRY THIS IF...

- the child frequently selects books that do not provide high-success reading experiences.

- social energy is building around books that the child is not able to read successfully.

- you sense it would stir up interest in a new author, genre, topic, or format.

GROUP SIZE

- Small group
- Whole class

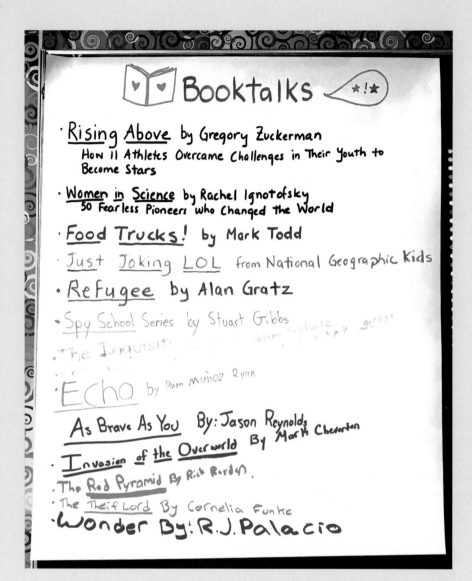

Booktalks *!*

- **Rising Above** by Gregory Zuckerman
  How 11 Athletes Overcame Challenges in Their Youth to Become Stars
- **Women in Science** by Rachel Ignotofsky
  50 Fearless Pioneers who Changed the World
- **Food Trucks!** by Mark Todd
- Just Joking LOL from National Geographic Kids
- **Refugee** by Alan Gratz
- Spy School Series by Stuart Gibbs
- The Inquisit...
- **Echo** by Pam Muñoz Ryan
- As Brave As You By: Jason Reynolds
- Invasion of the Overworld By Mark Cheverton
- The Red Pyramid By Rick Riordan
- The Theif Lord By Cornelia Funke
- Wonder By: R.J. Palacio

RELATED READING
Gambrell, L. B., & Marinak, B. A. (1997). Incentives and intrinsic motivation to read. In J. T. Guthrie & A. Wigfield (Eds.), *Reading engagement: Motivating readers through integrated instruction* (pp. 205–216). International Reading Association.

Annie book-talked a handful of books in Ed Urso's fifth-grade classroom, taking care to spotlight a variety of books including a joke book and a graphic, rhyming picture book about food trucks, alongside more complex, full-length titles such as *Refugee*. Ed and his students maintained the ritual, charting each day's selection for students' future reference.

NEXT STEP

Encourage the child to add titles from your booktalks to his Next-Up Book List. Once he has selected a book, return to the Volume Decision Tree on page 72 and answer **Diagnostic Question 2: Can the Child Procure a Copy of the Selected Book?**

Build Book Displays to Broaden Students' Choices

Books displayed on a rotating basis in the classroom provide a great opportunity to help students see connections between books and to highlight books students may not have discovered on their own. They also provide an opportunity to honor the interests and capabilities of all students in the class.

STEPS

- Be sure to include books your most striving readers can read independently even if this means borrowing from the library or another classroom.
- Set up eye-catching and inviting book displays in different places around the classroom.
- Be creative; there's no limit to the ways you can display books! Consider propping books on windowsills, the whiteboard ledge, or on a spinning display rack. You might also put a magazine basket in a cozy corner or set up displays on top of small tables or bookshelves outside of the classroom library.
- Consider displaying books from different genres and formats that focus on a similar theme (e.g., an expository nonfiction book about the planets with a book of facts about space and a biography of Katherine Johnson) or highlighting several books from a specific genre (e.g., a collection of hilarious joke books). And, of course, be sure the books you display are by and about people of all backgrounds. See Decolonizing Our Bookshelves on page 32 for details.

VOLUME-BUILDING FOCUS

- Access
- Choice

GOAL

- To build a reading community in your classroom
- To entice students into new reading territory
- To help students see different reading experiences one might have on a single topic of interest

YOU MIGHT TRY THIS IF...

- the child frequently selects books that do not provide high-success reading experiences.
- social energy is building around books that the child is not able to read successfully.

When color-coded bookshelves became a thing, Central School librarian Anne Corsetti captured students' attention with an all-orange display of old favorites and new releases in a variety of genres and levels of complexity.

SAMPLE DISPLAY

This thematic Space Display includes books from a variety of genres
(such as sci-fi and biography), formats (such as procedural texts and
graphic novels), and levels of text complexity.

TIP

- Invite students to curate displays of their favorite books the way indie bookstores feature staff
  members' picks. To encourage striving readers' participation, conduct Review Stack conferences
  first to remind them of the books they have recently enjoyed.

NEXT STEP

Encourage the student to browse book displays
and add books they are interested in reading
to their Next-Up Book List or take a copy to read
right away. Once the student is well matched with
a compelling book, give them time to read some
of the book. Then, return to the Reading Volume
Decision Tree on page 72 and answer
**Diagnostic Question 3:
Is the Child Invested in the Book?**

Read Aloud to Build an Inclusive Reading Community

Reading aloud a wide variety of books exposes students to genres, formats, and topics that they may not have selected on their own, ensuring that they have a balanced literacy experience. Reading aloud should be a daily practice that includes books even your most striving reader can read independently. This will go a long way toward promoting an inclusive reading community.

PREPARATION

- Choose a variety of texts to read aloud to your class.
- Make note of children who are dwelling in specific formats, genres, or topics. Select texts that they may not select on their own to provide them with a well-rounded literacy experience.
- Consider the spectrum of your students' reading levels and preferences, being sure to include books that your most striving readers can read independently.

VOLUME-BUILDING FOCUS
- Access

GOAL
- To expose students to a wide variety of reading experiences

YOU MIGHT TRY THIS IF...
- the child frequently selects books that do not provide high-success reading experiences.
- students are dwelling in specific formats, genres, or topics.
- social energy is building around books that the child is not able to read successfully.

GROUP SIZE
- Small group
- Whole class

Michelle Butchar's fourth graders love her daily picture book read-alouds, which she selects based on timely topics and student interests.

STEPS

- Set aside 10 to 20 minutes each day to read aloud to your class.
- Make a habit of reading aloud short texts like picture books, short stories, poetry, compendia, joke books, and news/magazine articles. Although reading full-length novels can be an enriching experience for your class, consider the opportunity cost of spending several weeks in one novel versus reading a multitude of shorter texts, which introduce children to various storylines, text structures, themes, and characters in the same time period.
- After you have read a text to the class, make it available to students to read independently.

TIP

- Keep a running list of read-alouds posted in your room.

Januari Pakrul makes it easy for her second-grade students to find books she has read aloud by keeping those titles in a designated bin in the classroom library.

NEXT STEP

Point out to the student that she can use read-alouds as inspiration for finding other books she wants to read. She can add those titles to her Next-Up Book List or use digital tools to search for books by the same author, or books within the same genre, theme, or format. Once the student has selected a book, return to the Volume Decision Tree on page 72 and answer **Diagnostic Question 2: Can the Child Procure a Copy of the Selected Book?**

Teach the Child to Find Next-Up Books

When students have reliable ways to find appealing books, they are less likely to experience stalls in their reading lives. This practice helps children discover and use reliable resources to find engaging Next-Up Books that will fuel their reading volume.

PREPARATION

- Familiarize yourself with and bookmark the website(s) you plan to show.
- Locate an Internet-enabled device for students to access online resources.
- Be sure students have their Next-Up Book Lists.

STEPS

- Say to students, *Knowing where and how to find great book recommendations is a valuable skill for any reader. Sometimes, when I'm looking for a new book to read, I get so overwhelmed by all of the choices that I end up walking out of the library with no book at all or with a book I'm not super excited to read. I've learned that there are lots of resources available to discover great books. Let's create a list of some of those tools together.*

- Brainstorm as a group various places students can turn to for book recommendations. Create a chart together, which may include the following:

  ▶ Online book recommendation and review platforms such as Biblionasium, DOGObooks, or Spaghetti Book Club.

  ▶ Read-alike recommendations from websites such as Goodreads' Readers Also Enjoyed or Amazon's Books You May Like features. Be sure to point out inside-the-book previews.

  ▶ The school or town library's online catalog.

  ▶ Recommendations from friends. (See "Urge Reading Partners to Make Recommendations," page 119.)

  ▶ Suggestions from the school or town librarian.

- Consider showing students how to access and explore any digital resources you have available. Allow students time to peruse the resource on their own.

- Encourage students to add titles to their Next-Up Book Lists as they come across books they are interested in reading.

- Repeat the process with each resource you share.

VOLUME-BUILDING FOCUS

- Choice
- Agency

GOAL

- To build students' ability to find compelling books
- To widen students' knowledge of available books

YOU MIGHT TRY THIS IF...

- a student relies on you to recommend books, but is ready for strategies that he can try on his own.
- a student does not have reliable resources for finding Next-Up Books.

GROUP SIZE

- One-on-one
- Small group
- Whole class

Teaching students how to navigate digital
library catalogs builds agency.

TIPS

- Consider spreading this practice over several days, introducing and exploring one or two sources per day.

- Think about sharing these resources with parents so they can help their children choose Next-Up Books.

- When a reader comes to you for help, refer him to the chart as a starting place to foster agentive habits. Be sure to follow up to make sure he was successful in selecting a title.

NEXT STEP

Give the student an opportunity to use various resources to find books he wants to read. Once he has selected a book, return to the Volume Decision Tree on page 72 and answer **Diagnostic Question 2: Can the Child Procure a Copy of the Selected Book?**

Discover Places Books Are Available

One of the best ways to help children develop agency is by helping them to discover where books and digital texts are available. When students have reliable go-to places for their reading material, they are more likely to move effortlessly from book to book and avoid stalls in their reading lives.

PREPARATION

- Familiarize yourself with your school and public library reserve systems. Ask students to bring their public library cards to school so they are ready to log in to their library accounts.
- Identify resources for digital texts and audiobooks. Many school and public libraries maintain subscriptions to a variety of digital resources.
- Locate internet-enabled devices for students to access online resources.
- Be sure students have their Next-Up Book Lists.

STEPS

- Say to students, *Knowing where and how to find books on your Next-Up Book List is an important skill for you as a reader. Let's create a list of options you can turn to when you are looking for a book you really want to read. Let's start with physical books.*
- Create a chart together, which may include:
  - ▶ Look in our classroom library.
  - ▶ Ask a classmate to borrow his copy.
  - ▶ Borrow a copy from another classroom library.
  - ▶ Reserve a copy from the school or community library's website.
- Role-play approaching the librarian or a teacher from another classroom to ask about borrowing a book.
- Show students how the library reserve system works. Allow students time to log in to their school or public library accounts to reserve a book. Explain the process for picking up a reserved book from the library (e.g., ask the clerk at the checkout desk, find the reserves shelf, and locate your book).
- Turn your attention to places digital texts and audiobooks are available. *Now, let's look at the many options available to you for digital reading and audiobooks. Let's start by logging into our school library webpage to see the options available there.* Give students time to practice logging in and navigating through the resources.
- Encourage students to be persistent in their search for copies of the books they want to read. You might say, *If you have trouble finding something to read, don't give up! Ask me, the librarian, or another teacher for help.*

VOLUME-BUILDING FOCUS
- Choice
- Agency

GOAL
- To build students' ability to find compelling books
- To widen students' knowledge of available books

YOU MIGHT TRY THIS IF...
- the book the child wants to read is located somewhere she can't easily access on their own.
- the child consistently obtains books from a single source such as the classroom library.
- the child routinely relies on you to obtain books for them.

GROUP SIZE
- One-on-one
- Small group
- Whole class

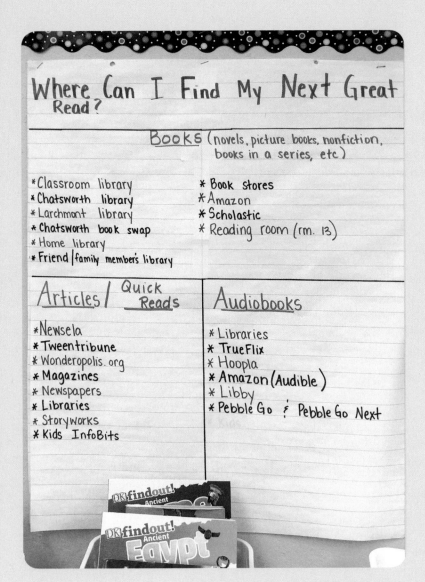

Where Can I Find My Next Great Read?

Books (novels, picture books, nonfiction, books in a series, etc)

* Classroom library
* Chatsworth library
* Larchmont library
* Chatsworth book swap
* Home library
* Friend/family member's library

* Book stores
* Amazon
* Scholastic
* Reading room (rm. 13)

Articles/Quick Reads

* Newsela
* Tweentribune
* Wonderopolis.org
* Magazines
* Newspapers
* Libraries
* Storyworks
* Kids InfoBits

Audiobooks

* Libraries
* TrueFlix
* Hoopla
* Amazon (Audible)
* Libby
* Pebble Go & Pebble Go Next

TIPS

- Spread this practice over several days, allowing students time to try various access streams for themselves.

- Consider inviting the school and/or public librarian to visit your class to help students access resources. Follow up with a class visit to the library.

- Ask the school librarian about the best times for students to visit the library to borrow books. Post these times in the classroom.

Fourth-grade teacher Lauren Dunlap keeps a chart in her room reminding students of the many places books are available to them. As a class, they add new access streams as they discover them.

NEXT STEP

Give the student an opportunity to procure a copy of a book on their Next-Up Book List and some time to read. Then, return to the Volume Decision Tree on page 72 and answer **Diagnostic Question 3: Is the Child Invested in the Book?**

Teach the Child to Use the School Library

The importance of a school library, particularly one staffed by a certified school librarian, cannot be understated. We recognize with sadness and frustration that many schools do not have a school library staffed with a certified librarian, but when a school library is available, the following are just a few of the many ways to teach students to maximize its impact.

BOOK-MATCHING

Librarians are master book-matchers. Have students bring their Book Maps to the school librarian and work together to identify books that will capture the hearts, minds, and imaginations of your readers.

SATELLITE COLLECTIONS

Many librarians will happily put together a small collection of books from a particular topic, genre, format, or level to live temporarily in the classroom. These satellite collections are particularly useful for striving readers.

DIGITAL RESOURCES

Encourage students to explore the wealth of digital resources school libraries provide. Ebooks, educational videos, audiobooks, and digital reference databases can spark curiosity, build background knowledge, and lead kids to new areas of interest. Teach them how to navigate available platforms to increase their book access.

CIRCULATION HISTORIES

Ask your librarian to share your students' circulation histories. They provide a wealth of information about students' reading histories and evolving interests over the years. Use the information to inform your book-matching efforts, and have students use it to reflect on their reading preferences.

CURATED COLLECTIONS

Share your students' niche interests with your school librarian and ask them to set aside space to house a specially curated collections of books for your most striving readers.

RELATED READING

Lance, K. C., & Kachel, D. E. (2018, March 26). Why school librarians matter: What years of research tell us. Phi Delta Kappan. https://kappanonline.org/lance-kachel-school-librarians-matter-years-research

Rotate Books Between Classroom Libraries

VOLUME-BUILDING FOCUS

- Access
- Choice

GOAL

- To ensure that all readers can access desirable books in the classroom library

YOU MIGHT TRY THIS IF...

- the classroom library does not contain books the child can or wants to read.

Sharing books with colleagues is a great way to maximize classroom library resources and ensure that every student has access to a range of appealing and varied texts. This practice is especially important when you have a limited number of books on a particular level, topic, format, or genre.

STEPS

- Decide which topics, genres, and/or formats you need to supplement with a rotating collection.
- Identify one or more colleagues with whom to share books. Have each one identify books she is able to share from her collection, as well as niches of need for borrowing. Put together collections of about 15 to 25 books organized by topic, genre, series, format, or level.
- Put a sticker on the back or inside front cover of the books indicating that they are part of the rotating collection (address labels work well). Discreetly write the collection's name on the sticker (e.g., Graphic Novels Set 1).
- Put the books in bins that can easily travel from classroom to classroom.
- Create a rotation schedule with the colleagues with whom you plan to rotate books.
- Rotate the books every two to three weeks.
- Consider borrowing from the school library, using Scholastic Reading Club points, or requesting funds from your administrators to purchase books.

TIPS

- Use caution when rotating books with a classroom from a higher grade level. Always be mindful of ensuring striving readers have abundant access to books they can read successfully.
- Avoid writing or putting stickers on the front cover of books, especially when noting a book's level. Children quickly adapt to looking on the back or inside cover of a book when checking to see where the book should be returned or what level it is.

When her students became fascinated by animals (particularly slimy and dangerous ones!), Januari Pakrul borrowed several bins from her second-grade colleague Kerry Daly.

NEXT STEP

Once the student has selected and procured a book to read, give her time to read some of the book. Then, return to the Volume Decision Tree on page 72 and answer **Diagnostic Question 3: Is the Child Invested in the Book?**

ENSURE ALL STUDENTS HAVE A LIBRARY CARD

You might be surprised to learn how many of your students do not yet have a library card. Help them fill out library card applications, then deliver them together during a class trip to the library.

BUILD RELATIONSHIPS

Invite your local librarian to visit your classroom in person or virtually. Have students role-play how to ask for a book recommendation, how to clear blockages on their accounts, or how to access resources like book reserves. If your striving readers know your local librarians' names and faces, they will be more likely to interact with them at the library.

PROMOTE PROGRAMMING

Striving readers can't take advantage of the public library's offerings if they don't know what they are. Regularly advertise your local library's programs to your students and their families. Many libraries offer free classes, homework help, book clubs, and other social gatherings, as well as passes to museums and other cultural centers.

MAKE TRIPS TO THE LIBRARY ROUTINE

The library is an essential field trip destination for students in all grades. Walk or take a bus to the local library, then set up a scavenger hunt to help students become familiar with the library's layout and offerings.

ACCESS DIGITAL RESOURCES

Explicitly teach students how to successfully navigate the public library's website. Students can learn how to reserve books, download audiobooks, and check the library's calendar for upcoming events.

CONNECT PARENTS WITH LIBRARIANS

Parents need to feel welcome at the library too. Parents who feel comfortable at the library will bring their children to the library. Consider hosting a parents' night or PTA meeting at the library and asking the librarian to be a guest speaker.

Promote Active Public Library Patronage

Albert Einstein said, "The only thing that you absolutely have to know is the location of the library," yet too many of our students have never stepped foot inside their local library. It is our duty to help kids recognize that the library is not a place reserved for the few, but a place that exists for the benefit of all.

Offer Private Reading Experiences With eReaders

We want all readers to experience the wonderful feeling of holding traditional books in their hands. When used thoughtfully, however, eReaders empower striving readers to engage with accessible books without the potential stigma of revealing the cover of a book their peers may have read years before.

EXPAND OFFERINGS

While we aim to build the most robust classroom libraries possible, we recognize that physical space and funding are limited. Many digital platforms allow instant access to thousands of titles. Be sure to familiarize yourself and students with digital offerings through the school and public libraries (see Discover Places Books Are Available on page 141 for details).

DIVERSIFY

Work with your school's librarian to curate a collection of digital books in the languages your students speak at home. Be sure to include texts that represent a wide range of cultures and experiences.

EXPLORE ANALYTICS

Many eReading platforms allow teachers to access analytic information, such as the number of books students have read and the number of minutes they have spent reading. Use this information to help understand your readers' interests and preferences.

SUPPORT STRIVERS

Allow striving readers access to eReaders that provide a discreet way to read high-success books.

eReaders allow students to enjoy books without the scrutiny of peers.

RECONSIDER DESIGNATED SHOPPING DAYS

Rather than a weekly shopping schedule, which may leave a student with nothing new to read for several days (or weeks!), consider establishing times during the day when the library is open to all for book shopping.

PROMOTE NEXT-UP BOOK STACKS

Encourage students to pull several books off the shelf. This way, they will have a stack of Next-Up Books waiting for them when they finish the book they are currently reading.

SET CHILDREN UP FOR BOOK SHOPPING SUCCESS

The classroom library can be challenging to navigate for some students. Take time to introduce students to the collection and help them to understand where they can find various books. Consider taking select students on an Inquiry Tour of the Classroom Library. See page 127 for details.

Provide Flexible Book-Shopping Options

The classroom library is often the cornerstone of a students' independent reading life. When second-grade teacher Kerry Daly noticed that James was reading The Magic Tree House book *Lions at Lunchtime* for the third week in a row at school, she realized that the routines we establish around book selection can enhance or hinder our students' reading volume. James was a "Monday Book Shopper" in the classroom that year, and, because of an assembly one week and a long weekend the next, he had missed his designated day to shop from the classroom. Kerry revamped the book-shopping routine in her class, allowing students to select new books as the need arose rather than on a set schedule.

Ease the Child Into the Text With a Book Introduction

Some books have features and/or structures that may be confusing to a reader. Set him up for success with a Book Introduction that teaches him how a particular book works. Taking a few minutes to explain a book's unique features and/or structure can turn a potentially frustrating experience into a successful one.

PREPARATION

- Before the conference, take a moment to familiarize yourself with the features and structure of a student's new read by flipping through the book and previewing the front cover, blurb, and table of contents. You might also read online reviews of the book for additional pertinent information.

STEPS

- Congratulate the student on his new book selection. *Yesterday, you decided to read Jedi Academy. How exciting to be starting a new series!*

- Ask about steps he has taken to orient himself to the book. *Tell me about what you've done to orient yourself to this book. Have you had a chance to read the back cover and flip through the book a bit?* If the reader has not oriented himself to the book thoroughly, guide him in doing so. *I also know that you are a big Star Wars fan, and that will certainly help you enjoy this book! There are a few other things you should know before you read this book.*

- Point out the particular features and/or structures of the book that will clarify and enhance the reader's experience. *As you know from your preview, this story is about a boy named Roan who dreams of attending Pilot Academy like many of his family members. Something interesting about this book is that it includes many different formats. There are letters, informational brochures, stretches of graphic narrative, and excerpts from Roan's journal, just to name a few. When you encounter these different formats, it might be a good idea to pause and think about how the part you read fits into the larger story.*

- Encourage the student to check in as needed. *As you make your way through this book, let me know if you have any questions or if things get confusing. I can't wait to hear what you think about this book!*

VOLUME-BUILDING FOCUS
- Agency

GOAL
- To set a student up for a successful reading experience by teaching her about the special features of a text

YOU MIGHT TRY THIS IF...
- the child is having trouble at the outset of the book, but you think he will be successful once he gets into it.
- a student is venturing into new or uncharted reading territory, such as a new series, genre, or format.
- a student is about to read a book with special features or a particular structure that is crucial to comprehending the text.

GROUP SIZE
- One-on-one
- Small group

The Notebook of Doom intersperses narrative text with a variety of illustrated text features and notebook pages that are key to understanding the story. A book introduction primes the reader to successfully engage with a book that has this type of non-traditional format.

TIP

- It is not necessary to have read the book before easing the child into it with an introduction. In fact, exploring a new book alongside a student will make the teaching that much more authentic.

NEXT STEPS

After easing the child into the text with a Book Introduction, give him time to read some of the book. Check in again after a day or two to gauge if he is having a successful reading experience.

If the child is not having a successful reading experience, turn to **Instructional Option 3: Support the Child in the Book** on page 149 and consider other ways you might support him in the book.

If the child is having a successful reading experience, return to the Volume Decision Tree on page 73 and answer **Diagnostic Question 5: Is the Child Making It Through the Book at a Reasonable Pace?**

Widen Access Through Audiobooks

Audiobooks are another way to increase students' access to books. Not only do they give children access to hundreds of titles that may not be available in your classroom library, they also enable students to enjoy texts that may be too challenging for them to read on their own.

EXTEND

Audiobooks open up a wide variety of options for all readers. They also provide a way for readers to build volume when reading physical books may not be an option, such as when traveling.

INCLUDE

Audiobooks provide a way for striving readers to engage with titles that are popular with their peers, allowing them to become part of the reading community.

SUPPLEMENT

Students may enjoy reading along with an audiobook or listening to the book after reading it on their own.

RECOGNIZE

All too often we overlook the rich tradition of oral storytelling in favor of the printed page. Some of history's most revered stories trace their roots to storytellers such as Homer, Anansi, and Aesop. Resist the urge to discount the rich experiences students enjoy when they experience a story auditorily.

RELATED READING

Dali, K., & Brochu, L. K. (2020). The right to listen: A not so simple matter of audiobooks. *Library Resources & Technical Services, 64*(3), 106–119.

Set the Child Up for Success by Building Background Knowledge

A reader might be drawn to books that contain unfamiliar cultural, historical, or factual content. When this happens, we should encourage them to do some research before reading. Fostering a habit of activating background knowledge before reading will not only set them up for success with the book they are about to read, but will be a skill they will draw upon for a lifetime.

PREPARATION

- Gather various media related to the book's content, such as maps, pictures, videos, accessible texts, and realia, such as replica artifacts or toy models.

STEPS

- Congratulate the student on choosing a new book. *I see that you've chosen to read* The Bicycle Spy, *a historical fiction adventure. I'm proud of you for spreading your reading wings and trying something new!*

- Explain the importance of background knowledge. *This story is set in France in 1942 during World War II. That is a time in history that you may not know much about. To get ready to read this book, you can build your background knowledge. That means that you can do a bit of research to learn about World War II before you dive into the book.*

- Demonstrate how to build background knowledge using various media. *Since this story is set in France, let's first take a look at a map of France during WWII. I notice that the country is split into Occupied and Free Zones. I wonder what that means. Let's look it up online.*

- Follow up by building background knowledge on any other important ideas that you suspect the child may not know a lot about. *It says in the blurb that the main character in this story helped pass secrets to fight the Germans. Let's look at this website to learn more about the French Resistance.*

- Alternatively, you could offer the student an accessible nonfiction book that they could peruse to build background knowledge.

- Point out to the student any features or content in the book that will help to build background knowledge. *You may have noticed that* The Bicycle Spy *has a glossary in the back. This will be a great resource for helping you to understand some of the vocabulary and ideas in this book. Chapter 1 will also give you some more background information about life in France during World War II.*

VOLUME-BUILDING FOCUS
- Agency

GOAL
- To set a reader up for a successful read by teaching them strategies for building background knowledge

YOU MIGHT TRY THIS IF...
- the child is challenged by a book's unfamiliar content or format.

GROUP SIZE
- One-on-one
- Small group
- Whole class

MATERIALS/ RESOURCES
- maps, pictures, videos, websites, and/or accessible, texts that you can use to help build a student's background knowledge.

Maps, pictures, and videos bring concepts alive, sparking students' curiosity and deepening their understanding. Consider purchasing replica artifacts, such as these WWII documents, about topics of particular interest for your students.

TIP

- Keep in mind, the focus here is to teach students how to build their own background knowledge by seeking out reliable resources. You don't need to give a full lesson on the content. Rather, give a simple introduction and point the student to resources they can use to build background knowledge in the future. Remember that students will continue to build background knowledge by reading the book.

- Take your cues from students. If they seem eager and ready to dive into their book, let them. Monitor their comprehension and respond if they seek background information once they are into the book.

NEXT STEPS

After providing background information, give the child time to read some of the book. Check in again to gauge whether they are having a successful reading experience.

If the child is not having a successful reading experience, turn to **Instructional Option 3: Support the Child in the Book** on page 149 and try other ways of supporting them in the book.

If the child is having a successful reading experience, return to the Volume Decision Tree on page 73 and answer **Diagnostic Question 5: Is the Child Making It Through the Book at a Reasonable Pace?**

DEEPER UNDERSTANDING

When characters, plot lines, and settings are familiar, readers have the mental space to think more deeply about what they are reading. They often come away from rereading experiences with a more sophisticated understanding of the story and a more nuanced look at the subtle plot points they may have missed during their first read.

RIGOROUS READING

Students experience rigor in texts that they are invested in reading. If we want students to have rigorous literacy experiences, we must do everything we can to help them find books they are motivated to read. As Kylene Beers and Bob Probst point out, "rigor isn't achieved by giving the student a harder text; rigor resides in the energy and attention the reader brings to the text" (2015).

UNFORGETTABLE CHARACTERS

When we rush children into longer and harder books too quickly, they miss opportunities to meet characters like Sofia Martinez and EllRay Jakes, who are part of popular culture.

NEW BACKGROUND KNOWLEDGE

A child who has watched videos and read books about a topic, such as the Alamo, will return to the first book she ever read on the topic with a wealth of new background knowledge. She will bring a deeper understanding of the broader context of the topic and have greater empathy for individuals she has gotten to know through her inquiry.

LIFE EXPERIENCE

Every day, children gain new life experiences that help them to understand old favorites in new ways. A child who returns to Dork Diaries after experiencing middle-school friendship drama understands the story on a much deeper level than she did when she first read the series as a fifth grader.

APPROPRIATE CONTENT

Children who move too quickly into more challenging books may encounter topics and themes that they do not have the life experience to make sense of. So, as you give them more challenging books, be sure children are mature enough to handle the content.

RELATED READING

Krashen, S. D. (2004). The case for narrow reading. *Language Magazine, 3*(5), 17–19.

Let the Child Linger in Familiar and Comfortable Books

Many teachers and parents are eager to move children into new or different reading territory. This is particularly true when children have spent weeks or months reading the same types of books; however, allowing students time to linger in familiar and comfortable texts has benefits that are important to recognize.

Orient the Child to a New Format

Sometimes a student is drawn to a book in a format that she has little experience navigating. Providing a quick orientation to the format will set her up for success with the book.

PREPARATION

- Select a book that has the features you would like to discuss with the student or use a book the child has selected.

STEPS

- Share strategies for navigating the format. For example, if you are working with a group of students trying out graphic novels, you might say to the student(s), *I've noticed that you are interested in reading graphic novels. This format is great for lots of reasons—the illustrations help you to really understand that story on a deep level, you get to do a ton of inferring, and they're just fun to read! When I first started getting into graphic texts, I had to learn how to read them. I wasn't sure where to look first, and I had no idea if there was a specific order I was supposed to read them in. Let's take a look at the first page. Just like in other books, you're going to start in the top left corner. Look at this frame first. Inside the frame, the general rule of thumb is to read the illustration and text from left to right and top to bottom.*

- Use your finger to track the places where you want the child to focus her attention. *Move on to the next panel like this (demonstrate with your finger), making your way across the page from left to right and top to bottom. Graphic novelists put a lot of care into helping readers navigate each page, so be flexible as you read and think about how the part you are reading fits into the larger story. Above all, think about whether what you are reading makes sense.*

TIPS

- Spend some time becoming familiar with formats such as graphic novels, manga, compendia, and infographics to help you understand why these formats appeal to students and how they work. Doing that will set your students up for successful reading experiences with those texts.

- Be aware that manga is read in reverse order, right to left across the page and within each panel.

- Take your cues from students; don't be too teacher-directed. Ask what they've discovered on their own about the ways their books work.

VOLUME-BUILDING FOCUS
- Agency

GOAL
- To set the child up for success with a format that may be new or unfamiliar to her

YOU MIGHT TRY THIS IF...
- a student is challenged by unfamiliar content or format.

GROUP SIZE
- One-on-one
- Small group
- Whole class

A general rule of thumb for navigating graphic texts is to make your way from left to right, top to bottom, across the page, as in this example from The Baby-Sitters Club series. The same generally applies to the text within each frame.

NEXT STEPS

After orienting the student to a new format, give her time to read some of the book. Check in again to gauge whether she is having a successful reading experience.

If the child is not having a successful reading experience, turn to **Instructional Option 3: Support the Child in the Book** on page 149 and try other ways of supporting her in the book.

If the child is having a successful reading experience, return to the Volume Decision Tree on page 73 and answer **Diagnostic Question 5: Is the Child Making It Through the Book at a Reasonable Pace?**

Encourage Families to Support the Child's Reading at Home

Families can be powerful partners in helping students develop a love of reading. The following suggestions are just a few ways they can support their children at home.

READ TOGETHER

Children of all ages benefit from being read to. Many books contain sophisticated themes and richer vocabulary than they usually hear in conversation. Reading books to children is especially powerful when they are invested in a title that they are not yet ready to read independently.

START A FAMILY BOOK CLUB

Talking about what they are reading is a powerful way to support children's comprehension. Pick a book and invite family members to read it together or independently. Come together to chat about things that were interesting, surprising, or confusing. A quick search for "book club questions" will provide hundreds of prompts to get the conversation started.

MODEL READING

Whether it's 30 minutes of household reading time for the whole family or sharing an interesting article from a favorite blog, when children catch the grownups in their lives reading, they internalize a powerful message about the value of literacy.

TALK

Rich experiences with oral language can have a powerful impact on students' literacy achievement. Engaging in discussions, debates, and informal chats helps children develop an authentic understanding of English grammar, learn about social norms governing language (e.g., how we talk to different audiences or when we want to persuade someone versus appease them), and develop vocabulary. With this knowledge, they will be able to tune into subtleties of the language used in the books they read.

RELATED READING

Trelease, J. (2019). *Jim Trelease's read-aloud handbook* (8th ed.). Penguin Publishing Group.

Share the Unique Benefits of Graphic Novels

Graphic novels have exploded in popularity during the last few years, and for good reason. This engaging and accessible format is deceptively sophisticated. A growing number of novels are being published in graphic form, making them a wonderful option for striving readers who want to engage with the story but are not yet ready for a traditional format.

VARIETY OF GENRES

Students are often more willing to try reading an unfamiliar genre when the text is presented in graphic format.

Fantasy

Biography

Sci-Fi

Adventure

Mystery

Historical Fiction

Realistic Fiction

INFERENTIAL THINKING

Each panel in a graphic novel represents a static moment in the story. Since there is little exposition in graphic texts, readers must make inferences to fill in the gaps from one panel to the next. In his book *Understanding Comics: The Invisible Art*, Scott McLeod helps us to see that sometimes the inferential thinking demand is low, as it is in the sequence on the left, while other times, it is quite high.

In this sequence from Varian Johnson and Shannon Wright's graphic novel *Twins*, readers must infer on several levels to figure out who is speaking, why they are so angry, and whether one person is yelling or three.

NAVIGATION

A common theme that emerges in conversations with striving readers is a preference for nonlinear reading. The layout of graphic texts allows children the flexibility to engage with the story in a sequence and at a pace that works for them. If you watch a child read a graphic novel, you are likely to notice her pause to closely examine the details in a specific panel or flip back several pages to reread a section with new insights in mind.

LITERARY ELEMENTS

The visual nature of graphic novels supports children as they are exposed to sophisticated literary elements such as flashbacks, backstories, foreshadowing, and figurative language. Notice how Kazu Kibuishi scaffolds readers' understanding of the following dream sequence from *Amulet: Prince of the Elves* by using a more subdued color palette and gradually changing the frame around each panel.

VOCABULARY

Illustrations often provide a visual reference for challenging vocabulary and concepts. After reading this panel from *Missile Mouse: The Star Crusher*, a child will likely have a better understanding of what it means to come from a long line of scientists. They will also be able to call to mind this image when they encounter that phrase again down the road.

Dream sequence from *Amulet: Prince of the Elves* by Kazu Kibuishi

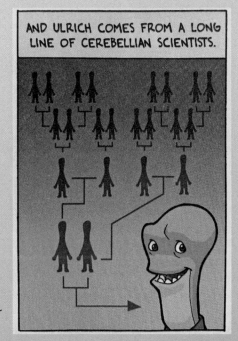

Missile Mouse: The Star Crusher by Jake Parker

RELATED READING

Jiménez, L. M., Roberts, K. L., Brugar, K. A., Meyer, C. K., & Waito, K. (2017). Moving our can(n)ons: Toward an appreciation of multimodal texts in the classroom. *The Reading Teacher, 71*(3), 363–368.

JOKE BOOKS

Joke books support short "bursts" of reading, which help students to accrue volume. They also promote reading fluency and help to create social energy as readers have the pleasure of reading jokes to friends and family.

COMPENDIA

Like joke books, compendia offer fun and engaging content, as well as the option to dip in and out of the book rather than reading it cover to cover. The flexibility of reading smaller chunks feels especially appealing and manageable to striving readers.

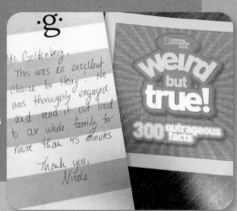

It might surprise some to learn that students often accrue more reading volume in compendia and other books with short bursts of text. Audrey Goldenberg learned that this was the case for one of her students when she received the note pictured here.

HOW-TO BOOKS

Students read for authentic purposes when engaging with how-to books because they are reading to learn a new skill or to create something. Additionally, they gain experience following steps and are exposed to technical and content vocabulary.

COMPILATIONS

When shorter books or series are compiled into one volume, this gives the look and heft of a more challenging text that striving readers often don't get to experience. Reading a compilation cover to cover builds volume and confidence for striving readers.

EXPOSITORY NONFICTION

Reading expository nonfiction builds background knowledge and vocabulary, and it often explores topics that kids are crazy about. The many text features—photographs, illustrations, maps, charts, diagrams, fun facts, etc.—give strivers entry points to information they might not discover by reading the words alone.

Promote Nonfiction Texts

Many teachers and parents elevate novels and other forms of fiction over nonfiction; however, nonfiction is a powerful format for all children. Thanks to the numerous graphic features that nonfiction typically contains, readers can glean information and build knowledge without having to read every word on every page. In addition to offering traditional texts (e.g., essays, news articles, information books), make a habit of promoting non-traditional texts like joke books and compendia, which are both fun and informative. Dismissing these books as "fluff" or low-level reading is a mistake. Most kids enjoy them, and they have powerful volume-building potential.

Take an Inquiry Stance When Reading Volume Slows

Even when a child is well matched with a book, his reading volume can suffer due to a variety of factors. When you notice a child's reading volume slow, take a moment to ask the child what's going on.

START WITH AN OPEN-ENDED INQUIRY

Mention that you've noticed that the child's reading rate has slowed and ask if he knows why. You might be surprised by the answer! While working on final edits for this book, Suzanne's son Shane mentioned that he'd rather not read *Refugee* (a book he was thoroughly enjoying) than have to stop-and-jot as his teacher required. The very same day, Maggie's son Cooper mentioned that he had abandoned *I Survived the Great Molasses Flood* because he kept losing his page when he took a break from the book. A bookmark for Cooper and absolution from accountability measures for Shane got them both back on a reading path.

CONSIDER SENSORY NEEDS

Students have different sensory needs. Some students may need a movement break before sitting down to read. Other students may benefit from using a cardboard carrel for privacy while they read.

OFFER EARPLUGS OR HEADPHONES

Some students need quiet when they read and are easily distracted by noise. Offering earplugs or noise-canceling headphones can be an easy solution to this problem. Don't assume that your students have a quiet space to read at home. Allow students to bring earplugs or headphones home if necessary.

PROVIDE FLEXIBLE SEATING OPTIONS

Ask about the child's physical comfort while reading. Not every reader is comfortable sitting up in a chair when reading. Offer flexible seating options, such as floor chairs, wobble cushions, stools, and standing desks.

Teach the Importance of Volume

VOLUME-BUILDING FOCUS

- Time
- Agency

GOAL

- To give students an understanding of the concept of reading volume and its importance

YOU MIGHT TRY THIS IF...

- the child has started moving slowly through his book.
- the child would benefit from learning about the idea of voluminous reading in a concrete way.

GROUP SIZE

- One-on-one
- Small group

Reading research isn't just for teachers! Share the research about voluminous reading in a child-friendly way to help students understand why reading is important and how it will benefit them. Armed with this knowledge, students can set reading goals to help them become voluminous, engaged readers.

PREPARATION

- Download the How Much Volume Should Readers Accrue Each Day? chart at scholastic.com/ReinventionResources. Be sure to group children reading books at similar levels of text complexity for this lesson, and avoid turning this practice into a competition or forum for comparison.
- Have students bring a piece of paper, pencil, and their books to the meeting area.

STEPS

- Introduce the concept of reading volume. *We know how important it is to read every day. The amount of reading that we do is called reading volume. Researchers who study reading have found that reading volume is super important! They know that the more you read, the better reader you become.*
- Pose a question to your students. *So we know that to become a better reader, you need to read. But how much should we be reading each day?*
- Display the chart. *This chart will help us to see approximately how many books we should be reading each day or week.*
- Explain the idea of reading rate. *A person's reading rate is how many words he reads in a minute at his normal speed. We all read at different rates, and reading faster is not necessarily better. Some third graders read about 62 words per minute.*
- Explain that books come in all different lengths. *Some books are longer than others. Of course, the longer the book, the longer it will take you to read it. Mercy Watson to the Rescue, for example, has just over 2,000 words in it.*
- Explain that a child's reading rate impacts how long it should take him to read the book. *So a kid who reads about 60 words per minute would make his way through Mercy Watson in a little over half an hour.*
- Summarize the conclusion and give students a chance to react. *So if you are reading for about an hour each day—including the time you read in school and at home—you should be able to finish one Mercy Watson book and start the next in a single day! What do you think of that?*

- Caution students that quantity should not take the place of quality. *We want to be voluminous readers, but we also want to be engaged readers. That means that we take time to think about the story, share favorite parts with friends, and avoid rushing through the book.*

- Follow up with each student. *Today, I'm going to meet with each of you to talk about your reading volume. Start thinking about whether you are reading enough each day. If you think you need to read more, we will make a plan together to help you reach your goal.*

TIP

- Understand that the point of this practice is to help quantify the idea of voluminous reading for students, but avoid letting quantity overshadow quality. We don't want students racing through books or becoming competitive about how much they read.

HOW MUCH VOLUME SHOULD STRIVING READERS ACCRUE WITH 60 MINUTES OF READING PER DAY?

WINTER OF GRADE	SAMPLE TITLE	AVERAGE WINTER FLUENCY FOR STRIVING READERS	LEVEL	WORDS IN THE SAMPLE TITLE	APPROX. TIME	APPROXIMATE NUMBER OF BOOKS (assuming 60 min. of daily reading)
1	The Lost Bear	In the winter of first grade, a striving reader in the 25th percentile reads on average **16 words per minute**	D	134	8 minutes	**7.5 books per day**
2	Don't Worry, Bee Happy	In the winter of second grade, a striving reader in the 25th percentile reads on average **59 words per minute**	H	342	6 minutes	**10 books per day**
3	The Infamous Ratsos	In the winter of third grade, a striving reader in the 25th percentile reads on average **79 words per minute**	L	2,422	30 minutes	**2 books per day**
4	Damonde Daniel Rich	In the winter of fourth grade, a striving reader in the 25th percentile reads on average **95 words per minute**	Q	5,217	60 minutes	**1 book per day**
5	Soccer Stand-Off	In the winter of fifth grade, a striving reader in the 25th percentile reads on average **109 words per minute**	R	11,353	100 minutes	**3 books per week** (Monday-Friday)

Hasbrouck & Tindal, 2017 (eric.ed.gov/?id=ED605146)

NEXT STEPS

Continue to monitor the child's reading pace as he makes his way through the book.

If he needs additional support making steady progress through the book, turn to **Instructional Option 4: Help the Child Make Steady Progress Through the Book** on page 162 and consider other ways you might support the child to finish the book.

If he is on track to finish the book in a reasonable amount of time, allow him time to finish, then return to the Volume Decision Tree on page 73 to answer **Diagnostic Question 6: Would the Child Benefit From Bringing the Reading Experience to a Close?**

SOFT START

Incorporate independent reading into your morning routine. Starting the day with 5–10 minutes of quiet reading builds community and eases students into the day.

BEWARE OF VOLUME THIEVES

Consider the value of every worksheet, activity, or project you assign. If you are not crystal clear about the purpose of the assignment and how it will help your students progress, ask yourself if the time allocated for these tasks would be better spent reading. Remove or limit assignments that do not have a clear impact on student progress and reallocate that time for independent reading.

How can we read more?

1. Find a new place to read.
   - outside
   - before school
   - lunch/recess
   - waiting for the bus/carpool/babysitter
   - when you can in other classes

2. Find a new time to read.
   - before bed
   - weekends
   - after other HW
   - in the morning
   - before other HW
   - before watching Netflix

3. Read something new.
   - Find a book you love!
   - Borrow an audiobook from me or from the town library
   - Read magazines and newspapers
   - Try a kindle/e-book.

4. Avoid other distractions.
   - Charge your cell phone (even if battery is full)
   - Give your cell phone to an adult
   - Airplane / Do Not Disturb mode

RECLAIM

Be opportunistic and capture every spare moment of time for reading. Students can read when they finish an assignment, while waiting in line, and after they pack up at the end of the day.

SELF-EDIT

Keep your lessons and "teacher talk" as efficient as possible to create more time for students to read.

Find Time for Independent Reading Across the Day

Time is arguably the most precious commodity in our school day. One way to squeeze in valuable minutes for independent reading is by looking across the entire school day for small pockets of free time. Five minutes here and ten minutes there add up to voluminous reading!

Create a Plan to Finish the Book

All readers fall away from their regular routine from time to time. If you discover that a student is progressing slowly through their book because they are spending less time reading than usual, help them to get their momentum back by creating a plan.

PREPARATION

- Give each student a copy of a calendar that they can write on.

STEPS

- Reassure students that straying from a reading routine happens to many readers, and is easy to fix. *We all have times when we fall out of our reading routine. When we move too slowly through a book, it can feel frustrating, and we can lose track of the story. When this happens, it's important to get back into our reading routine so that we can enjoy and finish our book. One way you can do this is by making yourself a reading plan.*

- Model how to make a reading plan. *I started reading* Child of the Dream *two weeks ago. A book of this length usually takes me a little more than one week to read, so I know it is taking me too long. I started this book just before the winter break ended. I was reading every day during the break, but since we've returned to school, I've had less free time to read. I'm going to make myself a reading plan to get back in a reading groove. First, I'm going to pick a goal date. I think I can finish this book in about five days.*

- Mark your goal date on your calendar. *Now I'm going to fill in times over the next five days when I can read.* Model filling in times on each of the next five days when you plan to read. *For example, tomorrow, I have to take my son to soccer practice, so I know that I'll be able read for half an hour while I wait for him. Wednesday will be a little trickier. I have to stay at school for a faculty meeting and then I have a doctor's appointment. I'm going to make sure I read at bedtime just before going to sleep on Wednesday. Let me write those times on my reading plan.*

- Give students an opportunity to make their own reading plans. *Now try making your own reading plan. Pick a goal date for when you think you'll be able to finish the book, then fill in specific times each day when you can read. Think about what your schedule looks like each day. For example, if you have dance practice on Tuesday, then consider that when you are scheduling your reading time.*

- As students complete their reading plans, support them as necessary.

- Let students know that they can readjust their plan. *I will check in with each of you tomorrow to see how your reading plan is going. Remember, you can always adjust your plan as you go. The important thing is that you are reading each day!*

VOLUME-BUILDING FOCUS
- Time
- Agency

GOAL
- To teach students how to restart daily reading habits by creating a personal reading plan

YOU MIGHT TRY THIS IF...
- the child has started moving slowly through their book.

GROUP SIZE
- One-on-one
- Small group

Reading Plan

Name: Jess

Title: Allies by Alan Gratz

Target date to finish: March 14

MY PLAN

DAY 1 Date: 3/10
Plan: Read for 1 hour before bed

DAY 2 Date: 3/11
Plan: Read for 30 minutes in the morning and 30 minutes after school

DAY 3 Date: 3/12
Plan: Read 20 minutes while mom makes dinner and 40 minutes before bed.

DAY 4 Date: 3/13
Plan: Read 1 hour before bed

DAY 5 Date: 3/14
Plan: Read 20 minutes after school 40 minutes before bed

DAY 6 Date:
Plan:

DAY 7 Date:
Plan:

THINGS TO DO THIS WEEK:

- bass lesson
- Coopers soccer Practice
  Make lunch
- My soccer practice
  Chores
-
-
-

scholastic.com/ReinventionResources

TIPS

- Remind students that in addition to scheduled reading time, they can also use "found time" to read. For example, they can read a few pages of a book while driving in the car or while waiting in the dentist's office.
- Keep in mind that some students benefit from making a daily or weekly reading plan to keep them organized and moving at a reasonable pace through their book.

NEXT STEPS

Continue to monitor the child's reading pace as they make their way through the book. Provide support as needed to help the child follow or adjust their plan.

If they need additional support making steady progress through the book, turn to **Instructional Option 4: Help the Child Make Steady Progress Through the Book** on page 162 and consider other ways you might support the child to finish the book.

If they are on track to finish the book in a reasonable amount of time, allow them time to finish, then return to the Volume Decision Tree on page 73 to answer **Diagnostic Question 6: Would the Child Benefit From Bringing the Reading Experience to a Close?**

Work With Families to Fuel Reading Volume Outside of School

Ensuring that students read outside of school is critical if we want them to accrue enough reading volume. We understand that life gets busy. Fortunately, there are many creative and flexible ways to squeeze reading into daily life!

SUGGEST RITUALS AND ROUTINES

Reading is more likely to happen when it becomes a habit woven into the daily routine. Encourage families to choose a time for daily reading that works best for them, such as first thing in the morning or just before bedtime.

IDENTIFY POCKETS OF TIME FOR READING

Encourage children to brainstorm a list of times through the day that might be available for independent reading. These might include sitting at the kitchen table while a grownup makes dinner or while waiting on the sidelines during a sibling's soccer practice. Look at children's after-school schedules across the week for days when extra reading minutes are possible.

KEEP BOOKS EVERYWHERE

Encourage families to keep books in the places kids spend time, such as on the kitchen table and next to the sofa. Kids are likely to squeeze in a few extra minutes of reading when a book is within arm's reach during unexpected moments of downtime.

PROBLEM-SOLVE

Work with the student to identify barriers to reading in their home. If the household is too noisy, encourage the family to purchase a pair of ear plugs or invest in a pair of hearing-protection headphones for the child to wear while reading.

BE CLEAR ABOUT YOUR GOAL

The goal of an initial home visit is to start a respectful and trustful relationship with your student and their family. You are not visiting just as a teacher, but also as a learner who wants to understand more about your student's life outside of school. Dr. Karen Mapp, who has done innovative work in family engagement at the Harvard Graduate School of Education, advises us to "see our families and community members as co-creators and co-producers of the excellent schools and learning opportunities that we want for all of our students."

BE WELL PREPARED

A home visit should not be entered into lightly. Before making one, take time to learn about effective practices of family engagement, which might include learning culturally sensitive protocols for home visits as well as examining your own core values and implicit biases. Take a small, literacy-related gift, such as a set of magnetic letters for the refrigerator or a bundle of books or magazines on high-interest topics. And keep the visit brief, no more than 30 minutes.

Powerful Partnerships: A Teacher's Guide to Engaging Families for Student Success (2017) by Karen Mapp, Ilene Carver, and Jessica Lander is an invaluable source of advice. Additionally, the Parent Teacher Home Visits organization (www. pthvp.org) has resources and training options for educators.

Fourth-grade teacher Alison Ivler forged a strong relationship with Victor's family, which was strengthened by the home visit pictured here.

FOLLOW UP

Build on the foundation of a successful home visit by following up with regular, personal communication with the family.

Make Home Visits to Build Relationships With Families

You can form formidable partnerships with families that will help children achieve success. One way to do that is by making home visits. Sheldon and Jung's 2015 study showed that students who received a home visit were more likely to have improved attendance and to thrive as readers.

Encourage Student-Led Booktalks

After students read a book they think others might enjoy, have them give a short booktalk introducing it to their classmates and highlighting some of its interesting elements.

PREPARATION

- Write a short booktalk to use as a model with the class. Have a copy of the book on hand.

STEPS

- Point out to students that booktalks have been an important way to share great books with the classroom community. Say, *This year, I have book-talked some of my favorite titles. Today, I want to give you an opportunity to give a booktalk about one of your favorites. Your booktalk should be like a quick commercial for the book. Grab your classmates' attention by including anything that makes the book interesting or unique, but don't give anything away—no spoilers! Let's take a look at some of the things you might want to mention in your booktalk, and then I'll give you some time to write your own.*

- Encourage students to name the title and author before sharing a little about the genre or format of the book and giving a taste of what the book is about. For example, *The action-packed adventure* Wildfire *by Rodman Philbrick follows Sam, a boy who gets separated from his group when a wildfire breaks out at his secluded summer camp. Sam has to figure out how to survive with only his wits and the clothes on his back.*

- Suggest that students finish with a reason why their classmates might enjoy it. *You might like this book if you're looking for a fast-paced page-turner.*

- Say: *Take the next ten minutes to write your own booktalk, and then practice sharing it with a friend. Tomorrow, I'll pick someone to give our first daily student-led booktalk.*

VOLUME-BUILDING FOCUS
- Choice
- Agency

GOAL
- To teach the key elements of an attention-grabbing booktalk

YOU MIGHT TRY THIS IF...
- students would benefit from book-talking books with one another.

GROUP SIZE
- Small group
- Whole class

- If a student is not comfortable speaking in front of the whole class, provide opportunities for her to book-talk in a small group or to videotape her booktalk and share the recording.

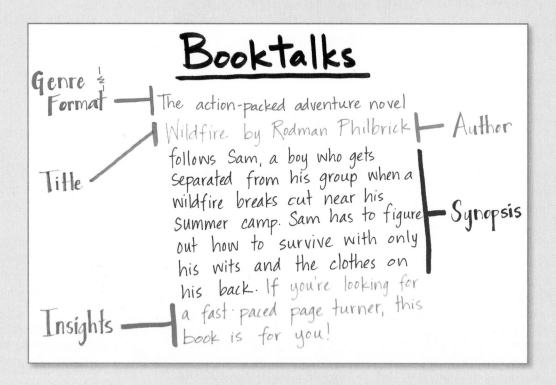

NEXT STEPS

Decide which students would benefit from your immediate attention. You can either:

After a child has given a student-led booktalk, if this has brought her reading experience to a close, return to the Volume Decision Tree on page 73 and answer **Diagnostic Question 7: Does the Child Have an Idea for a Next-Up Book?**

If the child needs to do something else to bring the reading experience to a close, turn to page 169 for **Instructional Option 5: Support the Child in Finding an Authentic Way to Bring the Reading Experience to a Close.**

Rethink Reading Logs

Traditional reading logs, in which students write in response to their reading, are ubiquitous in elementary school. But are they necessary? Consider why you are asking students to log their reading. If the answer is connected to accountability, think about whether it's necessary. If students are well matched with highly engaging texts, you shouldn't need external accountability measures. Consider the following alternatives to traditional reading logs.

TIME TO TALK

Give students a few minutes at the beginning of class to chat with a partner about what they read the night before to help them reflect on their reading and build relationships with other readers.

SHARE GREAT READS WITH OTHERS

When students finish a book, they can recommend it to others by giving a booktalk to the class, making a video book trailer, or recording their reflections on a digital platform such as Flipgrid.

TECHNOLOGY

Students can create a visual record of their reading by using a digital platform such as Padlet. They can look back on books they've read and reflect on their progress and preferences. Their notes can also be shared with families.

"CURRENTLY READING" WALL DISPLAY

Create a display where students affix stick-on notes with the title and author of the book they are currently reading. A quick glance at the display each day will enable you to identify who may need support making their way through their book at a reasonable pace, based on how quickly the notes are changing. This type of display also helps to spark conversations and recommendations among readers.

Third-grade co-teachers Jen Wiesner and Jen Cereola created this wall display to see what students are reading and to track their progress. As an added benefit, the ENL and reading teachers also began checking the chart and using it to confer with students.

Share the Benefits of Rereading

While teachers and parents are often eager for students to move on to new reading experiences, there are myriad benefits to returning to beloved favorites time and time again. Before encouraging a student to move on to something new, recognize and share with families the benefits of rereading.

DEEP READING

Since the child has already read the book, they are familiar with the content, structure, and characters. This frees up cognitive energy to pick up on nuances, make connections, and think more deeply about the story.

INVESTMENT

Readers who return to a previously read text know what they are getting themselves into. They already know whether the book is one they will enjoy.

VOCABULARY

Reading expert Carol Jago reminds us that the most authentic and effective way to learn new words is to meet them where they live (2015). It is through repeated exposures to words in oral language and authentic text that children add them to their vocabulary. Returning to a beloved text provides additional opportunities to encounter words that will be embedded into their long-term memory.

CONFIDENCE

One of the greatest confidence boosters for a striving reader is engaging in successful reading experiences. Rereading a high-interest book provides an opportunity for readers to feel confident in their reading.

REFERENCES

Alexander, K. L., Entwisle, D. R., & Olson, L. S. (2007). Lasting consequences of the summer learning gap. *American Sociological Review, 72*(2), 167–180.

Allington, R. L. (2009). *What really matters in response to intervention: Research-based designs*. Pearson.

Allington, R. L., & Gabriel, R. (2012). Every child every day. *Educational Leadership, 69*(6), 10–15.

Allington, D. (2012). *What really matters for struggling readers: Designing research-based programs*. Pearson.

Allington, R. L., & Johnston, P. H. (2002). Reading to learn: Lessons from exemplary fourth-grade classrooms. Guilford Press.

Allington, R. L., McGill-Franzen, A., Camilli, G., Williams, L., Graff, J., Zeig, J., Zmach, C., & Nowak, R. (2010). Addressing summer reading setback among economically disadvantaged elementary students. *Reading Psychology, 31*(5), 411–427. https://doi.org/10.1080/02702711.2010.505165

Anderson, R. C., Wilson, P. T., & Fielding, L. G. (1988). Growth in reading and how children spend their time outside of school. *Reading Research Quarterly, 23*(3), 285–303. https://doi.org/10.1598/RRQ.23.3.2

Atwell, N. (2014). *In the middle: A lifetime of learning about writing, reading, and adolescents* (3rd ed.). Heinemann.

Atwell, N., & Merkel, A. A. (2016), *The reading zone: How to help kids become skilled, passionate, habitual, critical readers* (2nd ed.). Scholastic.

Bates, C. C., McBride, M., & Richardson, J. (2020). *The next step forward in running records*. Scholastic.

Beers, K., & Probst, R. E. (2015). *Reading nonfiction: Notice & note stances, signposts, and strategies*. Heinemann.

Bishop, R. S. (1990). Mirrors, windows, and sliding glass doors. *Perspectives, 6*(3), ix–xi.

Bomer, K. (2015). With an air of expectancy. In Glover, M. & E. O. Keene (Eds.), *The teacher you want to be* (pp. 64–77). Heinemann.

Bridges, L. (2010). *RTI: The best intervention is a good book*. Scholastic. http://teacher.scholastic.com/products/classroombooks/pdfs/research/RTIresearch.pdf

Cervetti, G. N., Jaynes, C. A., & Hiebert, E. H. (2009). Increasing opportunities to acquire knowledge through reading. In E. Hiebert (Ed.), *Reading more, reading better*, (pp. 79–100). Guilford Press.

Cervetti, G., & Hiebert, E. H. (2015). Knowledge, literacy, and the Common Core. *Language Arts, 92*(4), 256–269.

Collins, K.; Bempechat, J., (2017). *No more mindless homework*. Heinemann.

Cunningham, P. M., & Allington, R. L. (2003). *Classrooms that work: They can all read and write* (3rd ed.). Allyn and Bacon.

Cunningham, A. E., & Stanovich, K. E. (1998). What reading does for the mind. *American Educator, 22*(1–2), 8–15.

Dahlen, S. P. (2016, September 14). Picture this: Reflecting diversity in children's book publishing. https://readingspark.wordpress.com/2016/09/14/picture-this-reflecting-diversity-in-childrens-book-publishing/

Dahlen, S. P. (2019, June 19). Picture this: Diversity in children's books 2018 infographic. https://readingspark.wordpress.com/2019/06/19/picture-this-diversity-in-childrens-books-2018-infographic/

Daniels, H., & Ahmed, S. (2014). *Upstanders: How to engage middle school hearts and minds with inquiry*. Heinemann.

Gabriel, R., Allington, R., & Billen, M. (2012). Middle schoolers and magazines: What teachers can learn from students' leisure reading habits. *The Clearing House: A Journal of Educational Strategies, Issues and Ideas, 85*(5), 186–191. https://doi.org/10.1080/00098655.2012.681281

Goudvis, A., Harvey, S., & Buhrow, B. (2019). *Inquiry illuminated: Researcher's workshop across the curriculum*. Heinemann.

Guthrie, J. T. (2013). Best practices for motivating students to read. In L. Morrow & L. Gambrell (Eds.), *Best practices in literacy instruction* (4th ed., pp. 177–198). Guilford Press.

Guthrie, J. T., & Humenick, N. M. (2004). Motivating students to read: Evidence for classroom practices that increase reading motivation and achievement. In P. McCardle & V. Chhabra (Eds.), *The voice of evidence in reading research* (pp. 329–354). Brookes.

Hammond, Z. (2020, February). Revisiting your library: Decolonizing, not just diversifying: Zaretta Hammond weighs in. *Research for Better Teaching Newsletter.* https://myemail.constantcontact.com/RBT-February-2020-Newsletter---Guest-Zaretta-Hammond--Revisiting-Your-Library--Decolonizing--not-Just-Diversifying.html?soid=1102010842973&aid=vgBPxU0hQV0

Harvey, S., & Goudvis, A. (2017). *Strategies that work: Teaching comprehension for understanding, engagement, and building knowledge, grades K–8* (3rd ed.). Stenhouse.

Harvey, S., & Ward, A. (2017). *From striving to thriving: How to grow confident, capable readers*. Scholastic.

Hasbrouck, J., & Tindal, G. (2017). An update to compiled ORF norms (Technical Report No. 1702). Eugene, OR. Behavioral Research and Testing, University of Oregon.

Jago, C. (2015). *Meeting words where they live: Help students enlarge their vocabulary through reading*. Heinemann. https://www.heinemann.com/pd/journal/Jago_Meeting.pdf

Janeczko, P. (2003). The Hardy Boys made me do it. In T. Lesesne, *Making the match* (pp. 51–52). Stenhouse.

Jennings, K. A., Rule, A. C., & Zanden, S. M. (2014). Fifth graders' enjoyment, interest, and comprehension of graphic novels compared to heavily-illustrated and traditional novels. *International Electronic Journal of Elementary Education. 6*(2), 257–274.

Johnston, P. H. (2013, March 14). Talk, decisions, and the intellectual and social life of the classroom community [Keynote address]. Mamaroneck Superintendent's Conference Day, Mamaroneck, NY.

Kohn, A. (2018). *Punished by rewards: The trouble with gold stars, incentive plans, A's, praise, and other bribes* (3rd ed.). Houghton Mifflin.

Krashen, S. D. (2001). More smoke and mirrors: A critique of the National Reading Panel report on fluency. *Phi Delta Kappan, 83*(2), 119–123.

Krashen, S. D. (2004a). The case for narrow reading. *Language Magazine, 3*(5), 17–19.

Krashen, S. D. (2004b). *The power of reading: Insights from the research* (2nd ed.). Libraries Unlimited.

Krashen, S. (2011). *Free voluntary reading*. Libraries Unlimited.

Krashen, S., & Ujiie, J. (2005). Junk food is bad for you, but junk reading is good for you. *International Journal of Foreign Language Teaching, 1*(3), 5–12.

Krishnaswami, U. (2019, January 17). Why stop at windows and mirrors?: Children's book prisms. *The Horn Book.* https://www.hbook.com/?detailStory=why-stop-at-windows-and-mirrors-childrens-book-prisms

Larrick, N. (1965, September 11). The all-white world of children's books. *Saturday Review,* 63–65. https://www.unz.com/print/SaturdayRev-1965sep11-00063

Lesesne, T. (2010). *Reading ladders: Leading students from where they are to where we'd like them to be*. Heinemann.

Mapp, K. L., Carver, I., & Lander, J. (2017). *Powerful partnerships: A teacher's guide to engaging families for student success*. Scholastic.

Marinak, B. A., Gambrell, L., Keene, E. O., & Duke, N. K. (2016). *No more reading for junk*. Heinemann.

Miller, D. (2009). *The book whisperer: Awakening the inner reader in every child*. Jossey-Bass.

Myers, C. (2014, March 15). The apartheid of children's literature. *The New York Times*. https://www.nytimes.com/2014/03/16/opinion/sunday/the-apartheid-of-childrens-literature.html?

Myers, W. D. (2014, March 15). Where are all the people of color in children's books? *The New York Times*. https://www.nytimes.com/2014/03/16/opinion/sunday/where-are-the-people-of-color-in-childrens-books.html

Miller, D. (2009). *The book whisperer: Awakening the inner reader in every child*. Jossey-Bass.

Morgan, H. (2013). Multimodal children's e-books help young learners in reading. *Early Childhood Education Journal, 41*(6), 477–483. https://doi.org/10.1007/s10643-013-0575-8

Neuman, S. B., & Celano, D. C. *Giving our children a fighting chance: Poverty, literacy, and the development of information capital*. Teachers College Press.

Neuman, S. B., & Moland, N. (2019). Book deserts: The consequences of income segregation on children's access to print. *Urban Education, 54*(1), 126–147.

Parrott, K. (2017, October 12). Fountas and Pinnell say librarians should guide readers by interest, not level. *School Library Journal*. https://www.slj.com/?detailStory=fountas-pinnell-say-librarians-guide-readers-interest-not-level

Pearson, P. D. (2014, May 9-12). *IRA Literacy Panel* [Panel discussion]. IRA National Conference. New Orleans, LA.

Peet, L. (2018). The end of fines. *Library Journal, 143*(15), 21–23.

Rodgers, E., D'Agostino, J. V., Kelly, R. H., & Mikita, C. (2018). Oral reading accuracy: Findings and implications from recent research. *The Reading Teacher, 72*(2), 149–157. https://doi.org/10.1002/trtr.1686

Strauss, V. (2008). Author works to prevent reading's 'Death Spiral.' *Washington Post*. https://www.washingtonpost.com/wp-dyn/content/article/2008/03/23/AR2008032301754.html?nav=rss_education

Sheldon, S. B., & Jung, S. B. (2015). *The family engagement partnership: Student outcome evaluation*. Johns Hopkins University.

Smith, F. (1987). *Joining the literacy club: Further essays into education*. Heinemann.

Stanovich, K. E. (1986). Matthew effects in reading: Some consequences of individual differences in the acquisition of literacy. *Reading Research Quarterly, 189*(1–2), 360–407.

Strauss, V. (2008, March 4). Author works to prevent reading's 'death spiral'. *Washington Post*. https://www.washingtonpost.com/wp-dyn/content/article/2008/03/23/AR2008032301754.html?nav=rss_education

Trelease, J. (2001). *Jim Trelease's Read-Aloud Handbook*. Penguin Publishing Group.

Von Sprecken, D., Kim, J., & Krashen, S. D. (2000). The home run book: Can one positive reading experience create a reader? *CSLA Journal, 23*(2), 8–9.

Ward, A. T., & Hoddinott, M. H. (2018). Riverkeepers: Strategies to keep vital streams of books flowing. In D. Miller & C. Sharp. *Game changer!: Book access for all kids* (pp. 32–34). Scholastic.

Wilhelm, J., Smith, M., & Fransen, S. (2013). *Reading unbound: Why kids need to read what they want—and why we should let them*. Scholastic.

CHILDREN'S LITERATURE CITED

Amulet: Prince of the Elves by Kazu Kibuishi (2012)

Animorphs: The Invasion by K. A. Applegate (2011)

The Baby-Sitters Club: Kristy's Big Day by Gale Galligan (2018)

The Baby-Sitters Club: Logan Likes Mary Anne! by Ann M. Martin (2020)

Bird & Squirrel: All or Nothing by James Burks (2020)

Crown: An Ode to the Fresh Cut by Derrick Barnes (2017)

Diary of a Pug by Kyla May (2019)

Do You Really Know Axolotls? by Ellen Rodger (2020)

The Dog: Best in Show by Apple Jordan (2008)

Dog Man: Grime and Punishment by Dav Pilkey (2020)

Dog Training for Kids by Vanessa Estrada Marin (2019)

Dogs of War by Sheila Keenan (2013)

The Doll in the Hall and Other Scary Stories by Max Brallier (2021)

Don't Worry, Bee Happy by Ross Burach (2019)

Dragon Masters: Fortress of the Stone Dragon by Tracey West (2020)

Dragon Masters: Future of the Time Dragon by Tracey West (2020)

Dynamonde Daniel: Rich by Nikki Grimes (2017)

Gaming Live! (2016)

Garvey's Choice by Nikki Grimes (2016)

Ghosts by Raina Telgemeier (2016)

High School Musical: The Essential Guide by Catherine Saunders (2008)

I Survived the Shark Attacks of 1916 by Lauren Tarshis (2010)

I Survived the Sinking of the Titanic, 1912 by Lauren Tarshis (2010)

The Infamous Ratsos by Kara LaReau (2016)

The Lost Bear by Michele Dufresne (2013)

March: Book One by John Lewis, Andrew Aydin, and Nate Powell (2013)

Missile Mouse: The Star Crusher by Jake Parker (2010)

Mystery Club: Mr. Wolf's Class by Aron Nels Steinke (2019)

The Notebook of Doom: Rise of the Balloon Goons by Troy Cummings (2013)

Ricky Ricotta's Mighty Robot by Dav Pilkey (2014)

Scholastic Discover More: Weather by Penelope Arlon (2013)

Secret Coders: Monsters & Modules by Gene Luen Yang (2018)

Shelter Pet Squad by Cynthia Lord (2014)

Soccer Stand-Off by Jane Maddox (2016)

Space Dumplins by Craig Thompson (2015)

Three Keys by Kelly Yang (2020)

Titanic by Jim Pipe (2007)

Twins by Varian Johnson (2020)

Young, Gifted and Black: Meet 52 Heroes from Past and Present by Jamia Wilson (2018)

Wings of Fire: The Dragonet Philosophy by Tui T. Sutherland (2013)

Zaha Hadid by María Isabel Sánchez Vegara (2019)

INDEX